NEW STUDIES IN BIBLICAL THEOLOGY 33

Covenant and commandment

Titles in this series:

An index of Scripture references for all the volumes may be found at http://www.thegospelcoalition.org/resources/nsbt

NEW STUDIES IN BIBLICAL THEOLOGY 33

Series editor: D. A. Carson

Covenant and commandment

WORKS, OBEDIENCE AND FAITHFULNESS IN THE CHRISTIAN LIFE

Bradley G. Green

APOLLOS

INTERVARSITY PRESS
DOWNERS GROVE, ILLINOIS 60515

APOLLOS
An imprint of Inter-Varsity Press, England
Norton Street
Nottingham NG7 3HR, England
Website: www.ivpbooks.com
Email: ivp@ivpbooks.com

InterVarsity Press, USA
P.O. Box 1400
Downers Grove, IL 60515-1426, USA
Website: www.ivpress.com
Email: email@ivpress.com

InterVarsity Press®, USA, is the book-publishing division of InterVarsity Christian Fellowship/ USA® <www.intervarsity.org> and a member movement of the International Fellowship of Evangelical Students.

Inter-Varsity Press, England, is closely linked with the Universities and Colleges Christian Fellowship, a student movement connecting Christian Unions throughout Great Britain, and a member movement of the International Fellowship of Evangelical Students. Website: www.uccf .org.uk

Unless stated otherwise, all Scripture quotations are from The Holy Bible, English Standard Version, published by HarperCollins Publishers © 2001 by Crossway Bibles, a division of Good News Publishers. Used by permission. All rights reserved.

Scripture quotations marked NASB are from the New American Standard Bible. Copyright © 1960, 1962, 1963, 1968, 1971, 1972, 1973, 1975, 1977, 1995 by the Lockman Foundation.

First published 2014

Set in Monotype Times New Roman

Typeset in Great Britain by CRB Associates, Potterhanworth, Lincolnshire

Printed and bound in Great Britain by Ashford Colour Press Ltd

USA ISBN 978-0-8308-2634-6 (print)
USA ISBN 978-0-8308-9777-3 (digital)
UK ISBN 978-1-78359-166-4

British Library Cataloguing in Publication Data
A catalogue record for this book is available from the British Library.

Library of Congress Cataloging-in-Publication Data
A catalogue record for this book is available from the Library of Congress.

P	21	20	19	18	17	16	15	14	13	12	11	10	9	8	7	6	5	4	3	2	1
Y	31	30	29	28	27	26	25	24	23	22	21	20	19	18	17	16	15	14			

For my students at
Union University

Contents

CONTENTS

Series preface

New Studies in Biblical Theology is a series of monographs that address key issues in the discipline of biblical theology. Contributions to the series focus on one or more of three areas: (1) the nature and status of biblical theology, including its relations with other disciplines (e.g. historical theology, exegesis, systematic theology, historical criticism, narrative theology); (2) the articulation and exposition of the structure of thought of a particular biblical writer or corpus; and (3) the delineation of a biblical theme across all or part of the biblical corpora.

Above all, these monographs are creative attempts to help thinking Christians understand their Bibles better. The series aims simultaneously to instruct and to edify, to interact with the current literature, and to point the way ahead. In God's universe, mind and heart should not be divorced: in this series we will try not to separate what God has joined together. While the notes interact with the best of scholarly literature, the text is uncluttered with untransliterated Greek and Hebrew, and tries to avoid too much technical jargon. The volumes are written within the framework of confessional evangelicalism, but there is always an attempt at thoughtful engagement with the sweep of the relevant literature.

This volume is a slightly unusual contribution to NSBT. It neither works out the particular theology of a biblical book or corpus, nor traces a narrow theme right through the Bible. Instead, it tracks through the Bible from Adam and Eve to the new heaven and new earth – a rather large and multilayered theme – the place of good works, obedience and faithfulness in the believer's life. For the Christian, to know Jesus, to confess him as Lord, entails obeying him. But how does this reality relate to a plethora of complementary themes? Dr Green addresses this question by soundings in an impressive diversity of topics: for example, the promises of a new covenant in Jeremiah and Ezekiel that anticipate a Spirit-empowered obedience, various relationships between the old and new covenants, and above all the centrality of union with Christ in addressing the relationship between justification and transformation. Along the way Dr Green interacts with various writers in the Reformed tradition, and with some contemporary thinkers (e.g. Henri Blocher, N. T. Wright). The canvas on which he paints is large enough to draw in a wide range of readers, all of whom will find themselves stimulated to think about these issues more precisely, even if they choose to demur from this or that element in his argument.

D. A. Carson
Trinity Evangelical Divinity School

Author's preface

The key issue in this book – the place of works, obedience and faith-fulness in the Christian life – has been of keen interest to me for many years. I am thankful for the opportunity I have had to work through these issues, and to try to make sense of some very thorny issues. I am also thankful to a number of places and people for the completion of this book.

Union University, where I teach theology, has been consistently supportive of my scholarship. The administration (David Dockery, Carla Sanderson, Gene Fant, Jim Patterson), my colleagues, our two wonderful assistants in the School of Theology and Missions (Christy Young and Marianna Dusenberry), and the Board of Trustees have helped in numerous ways. Thank you all. My former Dean, Greg Thornbury, was always a big encourager. Thanks, Greg. A number of persons read portions of the book, and I benefited immensely from the feedback. I am indebted to Desmond Alexander, Henri Blocher, Richard Gaffin, Simon Gathercole, Dave Gobbett, Graeme Goldsworthy, Scott Hafemann, Paul Helm, Gregg Hodge, Tony Lane, Peter Leithart, Bob Letham, Andy McGowan, Nick Needham, Matt Perman, Robert Sloan, Carl Trueman, Ray Van Neste and Steve Wellum. Mike Garrett was of immense help. He read the entire manuscript thoroughly, and brought it into conformity with the NSBT style. Thanks, Mike. Numerous conversations with Jonny Gibson have helped stimulate and clarify my thinking about biblical theology. Thank you also to my student assistants Brad Boswell, Dwight Davis, Andy Fortner, Ryan Linkous, Kelly Mikhailiuk and Eric Smith.

Phil Duce at Inter-Varsity Press has been very supportive and patient, and is a great editor. Thanks, Phil. It is a joy to have worked with D. A. Carson, who has shaped my thinking about biblical theology from very early in my studies. Thank you, Professor Don Carson. The copy editor, Eldo Barkhuizen, was outstanding. Thanks, Eldo. Significant portions of this book were written while at Tyndale House, Cambridge, England. Thanks to Peter Williams and all of the folks at Tyndale House for supporting biblical scholarship. My family, as always, have been very supportive. My wife, Dianne, and our three children – Caleb, Daniel and Victoria – are a constant source of encouragement and joy. Many thanks to my family.

Finally, I want to thank my students at Union University. You have been the recipients of the ideas in this book for a long time. It has been a joy to teach you, and I am thankful for you. This book is dedicated to you.

Bradley G. Green

Abbreviations

4QMMT	Halakhic Letter / Sectarian Manifesto (Dead Sea Scrolls)
ACCS	Ancient Christian Commentary on Scripture
BBR	*Bulletin for Biblical Research*
BECNT	Baker Exegetical Commentary on the New Testament
BNTC	Black's New Testament Commentaries
BRev	*Bible Review*
CCC	Crossway Classic Commentaries
EBC	The Expositor's Bible Commentary
ESV	English Standard Version
JETS	*Journal of the Evangelical Theological Society*
JSNT	*Journal for the Study of the New Testament*
JTIS	Journal of Theological Interpretation Supplements
NACSBT	New American Commentary Studies in Bible and Theology
NASB	New American Standard Bible
NICNT	New International Commentary on the New Testament
NIDNTT	*New International Dictionary of New Testament Theology*, ed. C. Brown, 3 vols., Exeter: Paternoster, 1975, 1976, 1978
NIV	New International Version
NIVAC	New International Version Application Commentary
NovTSup	Novum Testamentum Supplements
NSBT	New Studies in Biblical Theology
PNTC	Pillar New Testament Commentary
ProEccl	*Pro ecclesia*
RCS	Reformation Commentary on Scripture
SBET	*Scottish Bulletin of Evangelical Theology*
Them	*Themelios*
TNTC	Tyndale New Testament Commentaries

tr.	translation, translated by
TrinJ	*Trinity Journal*
TynB	*Tyndale Bulletin*
WBC	Word Biblical Commentary
WEC	Wycliffe Exegetical Commentary
WTJ	*Westminster Theological Journal*
WUNT	Wissenschaftliche Untersuchungen zum Neuen Testament

Introduction

Among the heirs of the Protestant Reformation there has been an emphasis on salvation by grace in general and *sola fide* (by faith alone) in particular. These were proper biblical recoveries during the Reformation era. It was important for the church to recover the central truth that we are justified by *God*, that this is an act of God's grace, and that faith – apart from works – is the means by which we are justified. It is striking that evangelicals have had to 'fight' the battle of justification many times, and this issue continues to divide Protestants and Catholics today in intriguing ways. Related to the question of justification is a key issue in biblical interpretation and evangelical church life: the nature of works, obedience or faithfulness in the Christian life. While evangelicals can generally agree that one enters into a covenant relationship with the God of the Bible by grace (even *solely* by grace) apart from works, there is often much more disagreement over how to construe the nature of works, or obedience, *inside* this covenantal relationship. My argument is that in the new covenant, works are a God-elicited and *necessary* part of the life of the converted person, a constant theme in the New Testament (John 14:15, 21, 23; 15:10; Rom. 2:13–14; 11:22; 1 Cor. 15:2; Phil. 2:12–13; Heb. 3:6; 3:14; 4:14; 1 John 2:3–6; 3:24; 5:3; Rev. 12:17; 14:12). In short, 'works' are 'necessary' for salvation because part of the 'newness' of the new covenant is actual, grace-induced and grace-elicited obedience by true members of the new covenant. When the New Testament documents are read against Old Testament texts such as Jeremiah 31:31–34 and Ezekiel 36:22–29 (cf. Ezek. 11:19; 18:31), this obedience is seen as a promised component of the new covenant.

The heirs of the Reformation have struggled at times to affirm the *necessity* of obedience conceptually while simultaneously affirming passionately *sola fide*. As Berkouwer wrote, 'One who has pondered the far-reaching significance of the "sola-fide" doctrine – justification by faith alone – is immediately faced with the question of whether this cardinal concept does not make all further discussion superfluous.'[1] My contention is that indeed there are resources within Scripture that affirm both *sola fide* and the necessity of works, obedience and faithfulness.

Berkouwer's note, perhaps, rings true with those of us in evangelical churches. We are rightly concerned to affirm a central truth like *sola fide*, but have not always articulated what it means to live obedience-filled lives, and to see practical faithfulness as a part of what it means to be a Christian. I suspect that some of our difficulty arises from simply saying that Jesus paid it *all*, while also saying that *we* must do something. This is understandable, but it is unwise not to address this issue. Indeed, there are solid biblical grounds for affirming a biblical theology of grace-filled and grace-elicited works, obedience and faithfulness as essential components of membership in the new covenant – that is, of being a Christian.

It is important to be clear what is being argued and what is not being argued. All throughout the New Testament documents there is the expectation of actual obedience. This obedience is generally linked to 'faith' or to loving Jesus truly. It might be possible to argue that some of these texts should be read as *commanding* obedience, without necessarily meaning that obedience is possible. We might call this a (hyper, although truncated) 'Lutheran' reading. But it is very unlikely that all of the New Testament commands or expectations of real obedience can be read that way. One is simply begging the question to read *all* of the New Testament texts calling for obedience in such a manner.

Also, I am *not* arguing that these 'works' or acts of obedience are somehow autonomous. I argue, following Philippians 2:12–13, that *we* truly do act, work and obey, and that at the same time it is God who is truly, efficaciously and actually eliciting and bringing about this obedience. I will also argue that this power for obedience is – ultimately – something that flows from the cross, from the gospel itself (cf. Heb. 10:10, 14), and is linked to our union with Christ.

The New Testament teaches that members of the new covenant are marked by an actual obedience, a real internal change and holiness.[2]

---

[1] Berkouwer 1952: 17.

[2] I am indebted to David Peterson and his excellent work *Possessed by God: A New Testament Theology of Sanctification and Holiness* (1995). He argues persuasively that NT teaching on sanctification emphasizes what is sometimes called definitive, or positional, sanctification. While I agree that definitive or positional sanctification is often in mind when the NT deals with sanctification, I argue that a real and transformative change occurs in the new covenant believer. The believer demonstrates actual obedience. This real obedience is rooted in and flows from definitive sanctification.

'Works' or 'obedience' appears to be expected in the new covenant. As John Owen writes:

> there is another kind of sanctification and holiness, wherein this separation to God is not the first thing done or intended, but a consequent and effect thereof. This is real and internal, by the communicating of a principle of holiness unto our natures, attended with its exercise in acts and duties of holy obedience unto God. This is that which, in the first place, we inquire after.[3]

Similarly, as J. C. Ryle wrote, 'Saving faith and real converting grace will always produce some conformity to the image of Jesus (Col. 3:10).'[4] Martin Luther could write of the one who trusts Christ, 'It is therefore impossible that sin should remain in him. This righteousness is primary; it is the basis, the cause, the source of all our own actual righteousness.'[5] Luther continues, 'the second kind of righteousness [real growth in holiness] is our proper righteousness, not because we alone work it, but because we work with that first and alien righteousness.'[6] Indeed, 'this [second kind of] righteousness is the product of the righteousness of the first type, actually its fruit and consequence'.[7]

There is a real and meaningful and necessary obedience – a changed life that includes *my* obedience – in the here and now. This is not a perfect obedience or perfect law-keeping, but it is *real* obedience, an obedience that (1) flows from the cross, (2) is a partial fulfilment of the promised blessings of the new covenant (e.g. from Jer. 31:31–34; Ezek. 36:26–27), and (3) is sovereignly and graciously elicited by the God of holy Scripture (e.g. Phil. 2:12–13).[8]

---

[3] Owen 1965, 3: 370.

[4] Ryle 2002: 132.

[5] Luther 1962: 88.

[6] Ibid.

[7] Ibid. 89. Luther elsewhere writes, 'If we believe in Christ, we are considered absolutely just for His sake, in faith. Later, after the death of His flesh, in the other life, we shall attain perfect righteousness and have within us the absolute righteousness which we now have only by imputation through the merit of Christ' (quoted in Piper 2002: 13). Luther says that after physical death, believers obtain 'absolute righteousness'. He does not clarify whether there is any *real* and *meaningful* and *necessary* obedience in the life of the believer whose sins have been imputed to Christ, and to whom Christ's perfect righteousness has been imputed.

[8] Turretin (1997, 2: 702–705) asks the question, in his *Institutes of Elenctic Theology*, 'Are good works necessary for salvation?' His answer: 'we affirm'. They are not required in a meritorious sense, but are nonetheless necessary for salvation. Turretin writes, 'Are they required as the means and way for possessing salvation? This we hold' (702). Indeed, 'Although the proposition concerning the necessity of good works to salvation'

The summary of my argument in this monograph is as follows.

Chapter 1 briefly surveys a number of New Testament passages where we see the centrality of works, obedience and faithfulness in the life of the Christian. I summarize these in several categories, which of course cannot help being somewhat artificial and imperfect.

In chapter 2 I attempt to do two things. First, I look at key Old Testament passages where a new covenant is foreshadowed and/or obedience from the heart is pictured as a coming reality. In particular, I turn to a number of Old Testament texts, primarily texts in Jeremiah and Ezekiel. We see the promise of a new covenant, and one of the features of this new covenant is the reality of Spirit-induced, efficaciously wrought heart-obedience. Secondly, I look at key New Testament texts that in some way affirm the reality of the new covenant and pick up on the Old Testament promises of a new covenant and the kinds of promises of obedience from the heart portrayed in the Old Testament.

What we see is that the New Testament writers recognize these same new covenant themes – that is, there is certainly something very *new* about the new covenant. And clearly, they see the new covenant as an existing reality during the first century. Interestingly, we see a number of passages and themes from the Old Testament, particularly from Jeremiah and Ezekiel, surfacing time and again in the New Testament.

In chapter 3 I broach some of the key biblical-theological issues a study like this must face. First, I raise the hermeneutical question of continuity and discontinuity across the canon – a question that can be dealt with meaningfully only over the course of the entire book. Secondly, I raise the perennial issue (at least for Protestants) of the law–gospel relationship, as well as the question of the salvation of

can certainly be misunderstood and misapplied, 'it can be retained without danger if properly explained' (702–703). Again, 'although works may be said to contribute nothing to the acquisition of salvation, still they should be considered necessary to the obtainment of it, so that no one can be saved without them . . .'. Turretin is clear: 'Although God by his special grace wishes these duties of man to be his blessings (which he carries out in them), still the believer does not cease to be bound to observe it, if he wishes to be a partaker of the blessings of the covenant' (703). For Turretin, Christ frees us to obey him: 'Christ, by freeing us from the curse and rigor of the law, still did not free us from the obligation to obedience, which is indispensable from the creature. Grace demands the same thing' (704). Works are necessary to the obtaining of glory, 'For since good works have the relation of the means to the end (Jn. 3:5, 16; Matt. 5:8); of the "way" to the goal (Eph. 2:10; Phil. 3:14); of the "sowing" to the harvest (Gal. 6:7, 8); of the "first fruits" to the mass (Rom. 8:23); of labor to the reward (Matt. 20:1); of the "contest" to the crown (2 Tim. 2:4; 4:8), everyone sees that there is the highest and an indispensable necessity of good works for obtaining glory. It is so great that it cannot be reached without them (Heb. 12:14; Rev. 21:27)' (705).

Old Testament saints. Thirdly, I raise the issue of how best to think of grace existing across the entire canon.

Chapter 4 takes up the issue of the relationship of the atonement to works, obedience and faithfulness. While it is imperative to think through the relationship of the atonement to the initiation or beginning of salvation, we *also* must think through the relationship of the atonement to the ongoing life of the Christian – an ongoing life that by necessity includes works, obedience and faithfulness.

Chapter 5 explores union with Christ, and its relationship to works, obedience and faithfulness. In particular, we are united to Christ by faith alone, apart from works, and because of this union Christ is being formed in us. So we should expect to see works, obedience and faithfulness in the life of the Christian.

Chapter 6 engages the thorny issue of judgment according to works. While justification is a past-tense reality for the Christian, there is also a future judgment according to works.

Chapter 7, the final and summative chapter, introduces several issues that have virtually begged for treatment throughout the book. In particular, I turn to the nature of the covenant in Eden, the believer's relationship to Adam and his transgression, and the relationship between Christ's obedience and our obedience.

Chapter One

The New Testament and the reality and necessity of works, obedience and faithfulness

Turning to the New Testament, it is an inescapable fact that works, obedience and faithfulness are central in the life of the believer. Indeed, in page after page of the New Testament we see that God expects his children to obey him. While it is impossible to treat in detail all the New Testament texts that deal with obedience, works or the transformation of the Christian, I outline fourteen key groups (explicated under the subheads that follow):

(1)	Loving or knowing God is linked with obedience	John 14:15, 21, 23; 15:10; 1 John 2:3–6; 3:22, 24; 5:3; 2 John 6; Rev. 12:17; 14:12
(2)	The 'conditional' nature of our future salvation	Rom. 11:22; 1 Cor. 15:2; Heb. 3:6, 14; 4:14
(3)	Christians must 'overcome' if they are ultimately to be saved	Heb. 10:38–39; Rev. 2:7, 11; 3:5, 12, 21; 21:7
(4)	The necessity of a great righteousness	Matt. 5:20
(5)	The requirement of the law being met 'in us'	Rom. 8:3–4
(6)	God will efficaciously work 'in' us, moving us to obey him	Phil. 2:12–13
(7)	The necessity of putting to death the old man, by the power of the Spirit	Rom. 8:13–14
(8)	'Faith' and 'obedience/works' used as virtual synonyms	2 Thesss. 1:8; 1 Peter 4:17; Rev. 12:17; 14:12; cf. 6:9

(9) We are truly judged, or justified, by our works	Matt. 7:21, 25; Rom. 2:13; cf. Jas 1:22–25
(10) The 'obedience of faith'	Rom. 1:5; 16:26; Acts 6:7
(11) We were created and redeemed for good works	2 Cor. 9:8; Eph. 2:10; Titus 2:14 (cf. 11–12)
(12) Faith working through love	Gal. 5:6
(13) The law affirmed; the law of Christ	Rom. 13:9; 1 Cor. 7:19; Gal. 5:14; 6:2
(14) Persons do the works of their Father	John 8:39

Luther argues that the obedience of a Christian is 'necessarily following' justification.[1] Calvin can argue that faith alone unites us with Christ. Our good works or obedience as a Christian flows from this union. Calvin can also say, 'Christ justifies no one whom he does not at the same time sanctify.'[2] Let us begin by looking at texts that appear to link loving or knowing God or Jesus with obedience. My goal in this first chapter is not to look in depth at all of these texts, but rather to illustrate that the importance of works, obedience and faithfulness runs throughout the New Testament. Certain key themes or passages will be treated in more detail in subsequent chapters.[3]

Loving or knowing God is linked with obedience

Loving or knowing God is linked (or synonymous with) obedience in a number of texts. Jesus says in John 14:15, 'If you love me, you will keep my commandments.' Likewise in John 14:21, 23:

> 'Whoever has my commandments and keeps them, he it is who loves me. And he who loves me will be loved by my Father, and I will love him and manifest myself to him' . . . Jesus answered him, 'If anyone loves me, he will keep my word, and my Father will love him, and we will come to him and make our home with him.'

---

[1] Luther, in public disputation with C. Cruciger, 1 June 1537; quoted in Rainbow 2005: 38.

[2] Calvin 1960: 3.3.1 (593); 3.6.3 (687); 3.16.1 (798); cf. 2.7.13 (361–362); 3.19.9 (840–842); 4.14.23 (1299–1300). All references from Rainbow 2005: 38.

[3] In particular, the issue of a future judgment and the future aspect or component of justification will be treated in chapter 6.

John 15:10 speaks in similar terms of commandment-keeping as a *condition* for abiding in Christ's love: 'If you keep my commandments, you will abide in my love, just as I have kept my Father's commandments and abide in his love.' Similar teaching is found in 1 John 2:3–6:

> And by this we know that we have come to know him, if we keep his commandments. Whoever says 'I know him' but does not keep his commandments is a liar, and the truth is not in him, but whoever keeps his word, in him truly the love of God is perfected. By this we may know that we are in him: whoever says he abides in him ought to walk in the same way in which he walked.

1 John 3:24 is similar: 'Whoever keeps his commandments abides in God, and God in him. And by this we know that he abides in us, by the Spirit whom he has given us.' As is 1 John 5:3: 'For this is the love of God, that we keep his commandments. And his commandments are not burdensome' (cf. 2 John 6).

A slightly different kind of text is found in Revelation 12:10–17. The 'accuser' has been 'conquered' by 'the blood of the Lamb and by the word of their testimony'. In 12:17, this same dragon is enraged, and makes war against the woman's children, 'who keep the commandments of God and hold to the testimony of Jesus'. Note that the keeping of commandments and holding to the testimony are spoken of, not necessarily as equals, but as in a symbiotic relationship. A similar usage is found in Revelation 14:12, which reads, 'Here is a call for the endurance of the saints, those who keep the commandments of God and their faith in Jesus.'[4]

In short, one common pattern in the New Testament is the link between loving or knowing Jesus and keeping his commands.

The 'conditional' nature of our future salvation

The New Testament texts that speak of *conditions* for retaining our salvation are of particular interest. A lot hinges on *how* one understands 'conditions'. We should not waltz into speaking of 'conditions', particularly in the light of the overarching story line of Scripture, and

---

[4] Aune, commenting on the link between keeping the commandments and holding the testimony: 'This is in essence a definition of Christian faith, in which the traditional commands of God, understood from a Christian perspective, are seen as complementary rather than antithetical to the requirements of faith in (or faithfulness to) Jesus' (1998: 709).

how much depends on how one thinks about 'conditions' when speaking of salvation.

However, the apparent necessity of 'conditions' in the Christian life must be faced squarely. Jesus says in Matthew 10:22, 'and you will be hated by all for my name's sake. But the one who endures to the end will be saved.' In Romans 11:22, towards the end of Paul's discussion of Israel and Gentiles in Romans 9 – 11, Paul writes, 'Note then the kindness and the severity of God: severity toward those who have fallen, but God's kindness to you, provided you continue in his kindness. Otherwise you too will be cut off.' Because certain Jews were cut off through their disobedience, Paul warns his Gentile readers that they *too* must 'continue in his kindness'. In short, continuing in the kindness of God is a condition for not being cut off.

Similarly, in 1 Corinthians 15:1–2, where Paul summarizes the nature of the gospel, he writes of 'the gospel I preached to you, which you received, in which you stand, and by which you are being saved, if you hold fast to the word I preached to you – unless you believed in vain'. Here again, it is necessary for Christians to 'hold fast to the word' if they are truly to be saved.

Two key passages in Hebrews illustrate a similar reality. Hebrews 3:5–6 reads, 'Now Moses was faithful in all God's house as a servant, to testify to the things that were to be spoken later, but Christ is faithful over God's house as a son. And we are his house if indeed we hold fast our confidence and our boasting in our hope.' And Hebrews 3:14 reads, 'For we have come to share in Christ, if indeed we hold our original confidence firm to the end.'

Both Hebrews passages seem to be getting at the same point: we must 'hold fast' (*kataschōmen*) our 'confidence' (3:6), or the 'beginning of our assurance' (3:14 NASB). This 'holding fast' is clearly a condition of remaining in the faith. It is something *necessary* and *essential* to the Christian life. Whatever it means to be saved by grace, to be justified by faith apart from works, we must include such passages in any sort of biblical understanding of salvation.

We should not miss a fascinating reality found in these passages in Hebrews. In both passages our present condition is (in some sense) contingent on a future reality. Thus, in Hebrews 3:6, we are indeed *now* God's house *if* we hold fast our confidence and boasting in hope. In Hebrews 3:14 we *now* share in Christ *if* 'indeed we hold our original confidence firm to the end'. That is, we can be said to be God's house (3:6) or to share in Christ (3:14) *in the present*, if *a future condition or reality comes to pass* – that is, if we hold fast our confidence and boasting (3:6) or if we hold our confidence firm to the end (3:14). I will offer a more thorough explanation of how to think of such 'conditions' later in this book (particularly in chapter 4), but these two passages are intriguing, because our current status or relationship with God is *in some sense* bound up with future perseverance or faithfulness.[5]

In Hebrews 5:8–9 the author writes, 'Although he was a son, he learned obedience through what he suffered. And being made perfect, he became the source of eternal salvation to all who obey him.' We set aside for the present what it might mean for Jesus to have 'learned obedience' (5:8). However one makes sense of that, the author teaches that through his death (and resurrection?) Jesus was made 'perfect' (5:9). And this perfect priest is 'the source of eternal salvation to all who obey him'. I draw attention to the obvious: Jesus is indeed the source of eternal salvation, but only *to those who obey him*. It is the burden of my argument to try to make sense of how best to construe the nature of such obedience.

Christians must 'overcome' if they are ultimately to be saved

Other New Testament passages speak of those who do, or must, 'overcome' (or 'conquer'; the Greek is *nikaō*). This is a refrain seen repeatedly in Revelation. For example, in Revelation 2:7 we read, 'To the one who conquers I will grant to eat of the tree of life, which is in the paradise of God.' In Revelation 2:11 it reads, 'The one who conquers will not be hurt by the second death.' Revelation 2:17 reads, 'To the one who conquers I will give some of the hidden manna . . .'. Revelation 2:26 reads, 'The one who conquers and who keeps my works until the end, to him I will give authority over the nations . . .'. In Revelation 3:5 we read, 'The one who conquers will be clothed thus in white garments, and I will never blot his name out of the book of

---

[5] Bruce, commenting on Heb. 3:6: 'The conditional sentences of this epistle are worthy of special attention' (1997: 94). Chrysostom, Theodoret of Cyrus and Theodore of Mopsuestia, each commenting on Heb. 3:14, make reference – in slightly different ways – to union with Christ. According to Chrysostom, Christians have been made to 'share in being' (with the Son). Theodoret of Cyrus sees Christians as 'joined to Christ the Lord'. Theodore of Mopsuestia speaks of how Christians have 'become partakers in Christ's "hypostasis" in that they have received a certain natural communion with him' (quoted in Heen and Krey 2005: 57). The reality of union with Christ, or our unbreakable relationship with the Son, will feature significantly in the central thesis of my argument.

life. I will confess his name before my Father and before his angels.' Revelation 3:12 and 3:21 similarly speak of those who 'conquer'. And Revelation 21:7 reads, 'The one who conquers will have this heritage, and I will be his God and he will be my son.' All these texts witness to a key central truth: Christians must 'overcome'. This is not optional, but is an essential component of new covenant life, the life of a Christian.[6]

It is worth noting in Revelation 2:7 that to the one who conquers, Jesus will 'grant to eat of the tree of life, which is in the paradise of God'. The first couple were expelled from the garden, and hence from the freedom to eat of the tree of life (Gen. 3:23–24).[7] But in the future, 'the one who conquers' will be given the freedom to eat of the tree of life. Commentators consistently link such 'conquering' with the cross of Christ. Hence Ladd, among others, writes that the victory being spoken of here 'is a victory analogous to the victory won by Christ himself, even though it involved his death on the cross'.[8] But it is *not* the case that the 'one who conquers' in Revelation 2:7 (and the ancillary passages) is simply Christ himself. Apparently, John has *Christians* in view, and it is necessary for such Christians to be 'conquerors'. Such conquering is related to the gospel itself, and to the Christian's relationship to Christ. That is, the Christian conquers by being bound up with Christ and what he has accomplished. Through faith alone the believer is united with Christ, and then a whole host of realities flow to the person who trusts Christ. It is only by seeing the believer's close union with Christ that we can avoid seriously misconstruing what it means to be granted the freedom to eat of the tree of life (Rev. 2:7). 'Our' expulsion from the garden is rooted in the first Adam's transgression, and 'our' future freedom to eat of the tree of life is bound up with the Second Adam's obedience. Although those who 'conquer' are *themselves* given the freedom to eat of the tree of life, and although *they* must conquer, it is important to trace out – and affirm – the relationship that exists between Jesus' conquering for us, and our eventual conquering. *The latter conquering*

---

[6] Regarding John's phrase 'the one who conquers', Caird says that the 'Conqueror' is 'one who perseveres to the end in doing the will of Christ (ii. 26), whose victory is analogous to the victory of Christ (iii. 21) . . .' (1966: 33). Similarly, Mounce writes that these 'conquerors' (Mounce: 'overcomers') are 'those who have remained faithful to Christ to the very end. The victory they achieve is analogous to the victory of Christ on the cross' (1977: 72).

[7] Whether they were eating of the tree of life *before* the fall is a separate question, dealt with below.

[8] Ladd 1972: 40–41. Cf. his footnote 21.

occurs only because we are united to Christ through faith alone in an indissoluble union.[9] We will return to the key issue of union with Christ (in chapter 5).

The necessity of a great righteousness

I now briefly point to several scriptures that speak of Christians having a great righteousness, or verses that make our forgiveness of others a condition of future salvation. For example in the Sermon on the Mount, Jesus says he has not come to abolish the law but to fulfil it (Matt. 5:17). After affirming the importance of the law (however one squares this with other aspects of NT teaching), Jesus says, 'For I tell you, unless your righteousness exceeds that of the scribes and Pharisees, you will never enter the kingdom of heaven' (Matt. 5:20). It is tempting to say, 'We don't *really* have to be righteous. It is speaking of *Christ's* righteousness!' But Jesus' point may be much simpler – all those persons who claim the name of Christ must have a great righteousness. It is *not simply* Christ's righteousness on our behalf that is in view (no matter how radically important Christ's righteousness is!). At other points in this monograph it is argued that our growth in righteousness flows efficaciously from God's grace, and is tied to our union with Christ. A simple appeal to 'alien righteousness' may cause us to gloss over an important component of the New Testament – *we must be righteous.* That is, when Jesus says that our righteousness must surpass that of the scribes and Pharisees, we have to do more than simply point to the righteousness of Christ. Leon Morris is certainly right: 'those who have been touched by Jesus live on a new plane, a plane in which the keeping of God's commandments is important'.[10] Donald Hagner notes that 'to belong to the kingdom means to follow Jesus' teaching'.[11] This is certainly the case, and it is my burden to flesh out what this might look like. D. A. Carson contends that righteousness is indeed required, although Matthew does not attempt 'to establish

---

[9] Bauckham 1993: 212. Although Bauckham is making a somewhat different point, and does not speak of union with Christ, what I am arguing is not altogether different from his thesis. Following M. Black, he suggests that Revelation might be considered a type of 'War Scroll' of Christianity. While Black emphasized *Christ's* role as the warrior, engaging in 'holy war' with 'the sword of his mouth', Bauckham wishes to emphasize *human participation* in this 'holy war'. I would agree that the message of the 'conquering' texts suggests that *Christians themselves* are to conquer. Everything hinges on how we link the 'conquering' of Christians to the 'conquering' of their Lord.

[10] Morris 1992: 111. While what Morris says is undoubtedly true, I wonder if he gets to the heart of the matter.

[11] Hagner 1993: 109.

how the righteousness is to be gained, developed, or empowered . . .'.[12] As has been argued, any righteousness that develops in the life of the Christian will always begin with the gospel – what has happened *outside* and *for* the believer. There is more to Matthew 5:20 than alien righteousness, as important as alien righteousness ultimately is.

Similarly, in Matthew 6:14–15 Jesus warns, 'For if you forgive others their trespasses, your heavenly Father will also forgive you, but if you do not forgive others their trespasses, neither will your Father forgive your trespasses.' Our future forgiveness is linked to our forgiveness of others. One might be tempted to gloss over such texts. Perhaps Jesus is using hyperbole to make a point, or he should be interpreted in a more straightforward manner: that part and parcel of the Christian life is to forgive others as Christ has forgiven us.

In short, both of these passages in Matthew appear to teach the necessity of obedience, or of righteousness. The second passage, Matthew 6:14–15, even seems to make our forgiveness of others a *condition* of our ultimate salvation – if we want the Father to forgive us, we must forgive others.

The requirement of the law being met 'in us'[13]

Romans 8:3–4 is treated in its own category due to its uniqueness. In Romans 8 Paul explains what it means to be under condemnation no longer (v. 1). In verses 3 and 4 he writes:

> For God has done what the law, weakened by the flesh, could not do. By sending his own Son in the likeness of sinful flesh and for sin, he condemned sin in the flesh, in order that the righteous requirement of the law might be fulfilled in us, who walk not according to the flesh but according to the Spirit.

Now, in verse 4, we might want Paul to say that the requirement of the law has been met *for* us. But he does not say this. Paul says that God sent his son to die so that the requirement of the law might be met *in* us (*en hēmin*).[14] As one looks across the New Testament, Jesus

---

[12] Carson 1984: 147.

[13] Lloyd-Jones 1973: 303.

[14] J. Murray, on Rom. 8:4: 'It is by the indwelling and direction of the Holy Spirit that the ordinance of the law comes to its fulfillment in the believer, and by the operations of grace there is no antinomy between the law as demanding and the Holy Spirit as energizing – "the law is Spiritual" (7:14)' (1959: 284). Cf. Rosner 2013: 121–124.

has unquestionably done something *for* us, and one of those things is that Jesus has been obedient *for us*. In the context it seems clear that our actual obedience to God, our minds being set on the things of the Spirit (v. 5), our being subject to the law of God (v. 7), and so on, all flow from what Christ has done for us. In Romans 8:4, Paul clearly says that the requirements of God's law are met in us. It would appear that there is an *internal* and *transformational* change that takes place in the Christian – a change that flows from the gospel. And the crucial point is that the cross of Christ leads to an internal change in the Christian: the requirement of the law being met 'in' us.[15]

God will efficaciously work 'in' us, moving us to obey him

Philippians 2:12–13 serves as the linchpin for the argument of this book: 'Therefore, my beloved, as you have always obeyed, so now, not only as in my presence but much more in my absence, work out your own salvation with fear and trembling, for it is God who works in you, both to will and to work for his good pleasure.'

The key here is that God *commands* something. Without making the Pelagian or Erasmian error of assuming that 'ought' always implies 'can', it appears that there is no reason to assume that the imperative 'work out' is simply given in a hypothetical sense. Paul expects his listeners to 'work out' their salvation. While God expects his covenant people to 'work out' their salvation, this 'working out' is something that God 'wills and works' in us for his own good pleasure. That is, it is not that God gives a command and then sits back. Rather, he both gives the command and then efficaciously moves his new covenant people to keep the command – and this divine action in no way minimizes the importance of human action. This biblical teaching would ultimately inform Augustine's writing in *Confessions*: 'Lord, command what you will and grant what you command.'[16] John Barclay is undoubtedly correct: 'Strikingly the divine work affects both the will and the action of believers: if even the will to act is attributed to God (whether as sole or as collaborative agent), the believers' agency is entangled with divine agency from the roots up.'[17]

A similar teaching is found in 1 Peter 1:5, which speaks of Christians 'who by God's power are being guarded through faith for

---

[15] Cf. Schreiner 1998; Stuhlmacher 1994.
[16] Augustine 1991: 202.
[17] Barclay 2006: 140–157.

a salvation ready to be revealed in the last time', which leads to the 'salvation of your souls' (1 Peter 1:9).

The necessity of putting to death the old man, by the power of the Spirit

Romans 8:13–14, a particularly interesting passage, reads, 'For if you live according to the flesh you will die, but if by the Spirit you put to death the deeds of the body, you will live. For all who are led by the Spirit of God are sons of God.'

Notice the apparent *condition* of future salvation: if one is living according to the flesh, one will die (v. 13). However, if by the Spirit 'you put to death the deeds of the body, you will live'. This passage is central to John Owen's classic work *Mortification.* In the second half of verse 13 Paul's argument appears to be something like this:

1. Christians must put to death the deeds of the body.
2. This putting to death (which is a human action) is done *by* the Spirit.
3. If one *does* put to death the deeds of the body, one will live.

As J. I. Packer has argued, contra a 'let go and let God' attitude, Paul's position is that one must engage in 'putting to death' the deeds of the body.[18] And whether we live or die appears predicated on whether or not we truly *do* put to death the deeds of the body. Now, we can either gloss over the imperative and conditional nature of this passage, if we are not sure how to square it with a theology of being saved by grace, or we might – as Owen does – argue that those in the new covenant truly *do* possess the Spirit, and hence *will* put to death the deeds of the body. Thus, if we are thinking canonically about the new covenant promises of Jeremiah and Ezekiel being inaugurated in the ministry of Jesus, then we should *expect* the Spirit-elicited and God-caused obedience, pictured in Romans 8:13 as 'putting to death the deeds of the body'.

'Faith' and 'obedience/works' used as virtual synonyms

Another set of passages are fascinating in that they seem to treat 'faith/belief' and 'obedience/works' as virtual synonyms. For example,

[18] E.g. Packer 2003.

in Revelation 12:17: 'Then the dragon became furious with the woman and went off to make war on the rest of her offspring, on those who keep the commandments of God and hold to the testimony of Jesus.'

Note that to 'keep the commandments of God' and to 'hold to the testimony of Jesus' are treated as corollaries, if not outright equivalents. Similarly, in Revelation 14:12: 'Here is a call for the endurance of the saints, those who keep the commandments of God and their faith in Jesus.'

Again, note how John, speaking of 'the perseverance of the saints', correlates those 'who keep the commandments of God' with those who keep 'their faith in Jesus'. Again, keeping the commandments of God and keeping faith in Jesus are treated as corollaries, if not equivalents.

Similarly, in Revelation 6:9 John opens the fifth seal, and sees the souls of those who had been slain because of God's word, 'and for the witness [testimony] they had borne'. The witness/testimony is something *maintained* or *borne*.

In 2 Thesssalonians 1:8 Paul speaks of God 'inflicting vengeance on those who do not know God and on those who do not obey the gospel of our Lord Jesus'. Again, to 'know God' and to 'obey the gospel' appear to be tight corollaries, if not equivalents.

Finally, it is worth noting that 1 Peter 4:17 does not simply speak of 'believing' the gospel – it is also something we must 'obey'.

We are truly judged, or justified, by our works[19]

It seems clear that at least in *some* sense our destiny is linked to what we do in this life. While the devil may be in the details, I am unable to see how we can avoid such a simple thesis. It is clearly taught in the New Testament and cannot be glossed over. Paul teaches in Romans 2:13, 'For it is not the hearers of the law who are righteous before God, but the doers of the law who will be justified [*dikaiōthēsontai*].' Rather than a brief digression by Paul, or a picture of a hypothetical opponent, Paul is teaching that there will be a judgment, or a future aspect of justification, in which works play some part. As Tom Schreiner has written, 'The need for good works to avert judgment is an integral part of Paul's gospel.'[20]

---

[19] See Schreiner 1993a.
[20] Schreiner 2001: 470.

The questions of future judgment according to works and whether/ how works relate to justification in some way are examined in chapter 6.

The 'obedience of faith'

Another group of texts speak of the 'obedience of faith'. The key passages are Romans 1:5 and 16:26. Romans 1:5 reads, 'through whom we have received grace and apostleship to bring about the obedience of faith for the sake of his name among all the nations'. Romans 16:26 reads, 'but has now been disclosed and through the prophetic writings has been made known to all nations, according to the command of the eternal God, to bring about the obedience of faith . . .'. The key exegetical issue is whether 'obedience of faith' (*hypakoēn pisteōs*) refers to an obedience that has its *source* in faith, or *is* faith. A similar wording is found in Acts 6:7, where Luke speaks of the spread of the gospel, and how many priests were becoming 'obedient to the faith' (*hypēkouon tē pistei*).

Douglas Moo has recently argued that the 'obedience of faith' should ultimately be seen in a twofold non-reductionist manner. The 'obedience of faith' is both the obedience that is faith, and the obedience that flows from faith.[21] The meaning of 'obedience of faith' in Romans, then, may well provide a basis for seeing obedience in the new covenant as 'obedience that flows from faith'.

We were created and redeemed for good works

A number of texts teach that God's purpose in creating and/or redeeming us was that we might do good works. Thus Ephesians 2:10 says, 'For we are his workmanship, created in Christ Jesus for good works [*ergois agathois*], which God prepared beforehand, that we should walk in them.'

Similarly, Titus 2:14 speaks of Jesus, 'who gave himself for us to redeem us from all lawlessness and to purify for himself a people for his own possession who are zealous for good works [*kalōn ergōn*]'.

In both of these passages good works/deeds are a part of God's plan or purposes – we are created for good works in Ephesians 2:10, and are redeemed that we might be zealous for good works/deeds in Titus 2:14. Titus 2:11 is especially interesting because of the explicit

---

[21] Moo 2007.

linking of the 'grace of God' to a changed life. Hence Paul writes that 'the grace of God has appeared, bringing salvation for all people'; assuredly, this includes the atoning work of Christ, particularly given the mention of this in 2:13–14 ('Jesus Christ, who gave himself for us'). And this grace has appeared, 'bringing salvation for all people, training us to renounce ungodliness and worldly passions, and to live self-controlled, upright, and godly lives in the present age' (v. 12). In short, as Paul sees it, 'the grace of God' (manifested in the atoning work of Christ – 2:14) trains us to live different lives than we lived before we were the beneficiaries of Christ's atoning work.

Faith working through love

Galatians 5:6 is a key text that has resurfaced often in Protestant–Catholic polemics. Paul writes, 'For in Christ Jesus neither circumcision nor uncircumcision counts for anything, but only faith working through love.' This text is a staple of Roman Catholic polemics that articulate an understanding of 'working faith', often portrayed in contradistinction to Protestant understandings of the nature of faith. But evangelicals have no reason to be squeamish about Galatians 5:6. Throughout his writings Paul makes the point that in the new covenant what matters is having a circumcised heart, and that heart-obedience flows from a circumcised heart. In Romans 2:25–29, Paul can be understood to say that it is the true Jew (not quite, but almost Paul's phraseology!) who obeys God's commands, for the true Jew has a circumcised heart. When Paul in Galatians 5:6 speaks of faith working through love, he is simply stating what is common across the entire canon: biblical faith is a working faith.

The law affirmed; the law of Christ

Another general type of text in the New Testament affirms the law (even if transposed into a NT key). For example, Paul in Romans 13 makes recourse to the Ten Commandments in explicating the nature of Christian love. He refers to four of the Commandments *explicitly* ('You shall not commit adultery, You shall not murder, You shall not steal, You shall not covet', v. 9), but then refers to 'any other commandment' and surmises that all such commandments are 'summed up in this word: "You shall love your neighbour as yourself"' (v. 9).

In writing to the troubled church at Corinth, Paul makes a rather stunning statement. He is encouraging the recipients to 'lead the life that the Lord has assigned' to them (1 Cor. 7:17). That is the key issue, for circumcision is simply not important in the new covenant era. Paul writes, 'For neither circumcision counts for anything nor uncircumcision, but keeping the commands of God' (1 Cor. 7:19).[22] If we practice a certain kind of Protestant polemic, we may find it striking that Paul does not contrast physical circumcision and spiritual circumcision (which of course he does elsewhere), or contrast something *simply* found in the Old Testament and *particularly* found in the New Testament. But he does not do that. Rather, he here makes the point that what is *truly* important is keeping the commandments of God. So, however one construes the newness of the new covenant, and however one ultimately makes sense of the advance in the history of redemption in moving from old covenant to new covenant, it is clearly the case that keeping the commands of God is central across the entire canon.

Finally, among a number of similar passages, attention should be drawn to a couple of passages in Galatians and a related passage in Matthew. Paul, in speaking of true Christian freedom, tells the Galatians that freedom must be used in accord with Christian love. So, he writes, 'through love serve one another' (Gal. 5:13). He continues, 'For the whole law is fulfilled in one word: "You shall love your neighbour as yourself"' (Gal. 5:14). Paul of course is saying something remarkably similar to Jesus' teaching in Matthew 22. When Jesus is asked about the greatest command in the law, he answers that one must love God and neighbour (Matt. 22:36–39). Indeed, 'On these two commandments depend all the Law and the Prophets' (Matt. 22:40).

In Galatians 6:2 Paul speaks of the 'law of Christ' (*ton nomon tou Christou*). This teaching is most assuredly along the lines of the passages in Galatians 5 and Matthew 22 just discussed. Paul commands the Galatians to 'bear one another's burdens, and so fulfil the law of Christ' (Gal. 6:2). Surely, such bearing of burdens is simply one way of loving one's neighbour? And it is in bearing another person's burdens that one is fulfilling the law of Christ. We find similar echoes in John 13:34, where Jesus gives a 'new commandment', which is 'that you love another'. Likewise, we read in 1 John 4:21, 'And this commandment we have from him: whoever loves God must also love his brother.'

---

[22] Rosner 2013 (his book takes this verse as its subtitle).

Persons do the works of their Father

This passage could arguably be in one of the other categories, but it is so striking that it deserves separate mention here. I draw attention to a pattern seen in John 8. In a lengthy exchange with certain Jews, Jesus makes claims about the nature of works (sometimes directly, and sometimes indirectly). In John 8:31–32 Jesus teaches, 'If you abide in my word, you are truly my disciples, and you will know the truth, and the truth will set you free.' In the light of other passages in John (14:15–24 and 15:1–17, where abiding in Jesus, bearing fruit and keeping Jesus' commandments are closely linked), abiding in Jesus' words implies the necessity of works, obedience and faithfulness.

But things get particularly interesting in John 8:39–44. Jesus has just claimed that these Jews *do* what they have heard from their father (John 8:38). These Jews answer that *Abraham* is their father (John 8:39). Jesus responds, and this is the key, 'If you were Abraham's children, you would be doing the works Abraham did' (John 8:39). Jesus' continued indictment in John 8:41 is that these Jews 'are doing the works your father did'. And then Jesus continues in John 8:42, 'If God were your Father, you would love me.' And then in John 8:44, 'your will is to do your father's desires'.

From Jesus' cutting criticism of these Jews, at least two clear truths emerge. First, it appears that, as Jesus sees it, *persons do the works of their Father*, whoever that Father is. These Jews do the work of *their* father, whom Jesus claims is the Devil (John 8:44). According to Jesus, works are simply part and parcel of life. People will *always* do the works of their father. The *key* question is, who is our father? Secondly, we find here an allusion (at least) to a truth very clearly taught elsewhere in John. In John 8:42 Jesus teaches, 'If God were your Father, you would love me.' So, if (1) to have God as Father means one will do the works of God, and if (2) to have God as Father means one will love Jesus (taught in John 8:44), then it follows that to love Jesus is to do the works of the Father.

Excursus: works of the law

For some time, one of the most contested issues in Pauline studies has been how to understand the phrase 'works of the law' (*ergōn nomou*). This phrase occurs eight times in the New Testament:

Rom. 3:20: 'For by *works of the law* no human being will be justified in his sight, since through the law comes knowledge of sin.'

Rom. 3:28: 'For we hold that one is justified by faith apart from *works of the law.*'

Gal. 2:15–16: 'We ourselves are Jews by birth and not Gentile sinners; yet we know that a person is not justified by *works of the law* but through faith in Jesus Christ, so we also have believed in Christ Jesus, in order to be justified by faith in Christ and not by *works of the law*, because by *works of the law* no one will be justified.'

Gal. 3:2: 'Let me ask you only this: Did you receive the Spirit by *works of the law* or by hearing with faith?'

Gal. 3:5: 'Does he who supplies the Spirit to you and works miracles among you do so by *works of the law*, or by hearing with faith?'

Gal. 3:10: 'For all who rely on *works of the law* are under a curse; for it is written, "Cursed be everyone who does not abide by all things written in the Book of the Law, and do them."'

Tom Schreiner has outlined five ways scholars have interpreted this phrase.[23]

---

[23] These five general positions as Schreiner (1993b: 975–976) lists them:

(1) *Nomistic Service*: identified with scholars such as E. Lohmeyer, where the emphasis is on 'the religious context in which the Law is kept'. J. B. Tyson emphasizes 'the condition of life under Torah, particularly the demand to observe food laws and to be circumcised'. Here, the reason the 'works of the law' are criticized is not because such works are too difficult, but because with the coming of Christ in the new covenant, we live in a different era in which such Jew–Gentile distinctions are no longer valid.

(2) *Jewish Nationalism*: J. D. G. Dunn sees the 'works of the law' as 'identity markers', such as circumcision, food laws, and Sabbath-keeping – for these separated Jews and Gentiles. The 'problem was with Jewish *nationalism* and *particularism*, not with *legalism* or *activism*' (emphases original).

(3) *Legalism*: D. Fuller contends that Paul does not argue that no one can obey the law, for the law is a 'law of faith'. Paul's polemic is against a distortion of the law, not against the law itself.

(4) *Subjective Genitive*: L. Gaston suggests that 'works of the law' is a subjective genitive, and hence denotes 'works which the law does'. What the law does – ultimately – is to produce sin and unrighteousness, which cannot justify someone.

(5) *Human Inability*: S. Westerholm says that legalism per se is not the issue, but rather human inability to obey the law.

The thesis of this monograph is not dependent on these or any other interpretations of 'works of the law'. It seems most natural to understand 'works of the law' to refer to something like 'works the law requires, or calls for'; that is, works done in service to God. However, the burden here is to explore why works are central to the Christian life, and how works relate to such truths as justification and to what Jesus has done for us.

Conclusion

I chose in this chapter to look briefly at a large number of scriptures, to make a basic point: works, obedience and faithfulness are central to the life of the new covenant believer. I have not attempted to work out all of the details of how works, obedience and faithfulness relate to a biblical understanding of salvation in general, and to biblical understandings of justification, sanctification and glorification in particular. To make sense of such key New Testament passages, we must understand them against a certain biblical-theological matrix: the burden of the next chapter.

Schreiner's own position is that Paul spoke against 'works of the law' for three reasons: (1) No one can obey the law perfectly, (2) any attempt to obey the law to gain righteousness is legalistic and contrary to the principle of faith, and (3) there is a salvation-historical shift that took effect with the death and resurrection of Christ.

Cf. more recently Schreiner 2008: 526–527.

Chapter Two

Obedience, works and faithfulness: moving from Old Testament to New Testament

The purpose of this chapter is to look at an overarching theme (or set of themes) in the Christian canon – to provide a biblical backdrop against which to make sense of the heart of the first chapter: works, obedience and faithfulness are central to the life of the new covenant believer.

First, I survey key texts in the Old Testament that repeatedly speak of a future day when, through the Spirit, heart-obedience will be seen in God's people. This heart-obedience is a result of God's grace and takes place through the power and work of the Holy Spirit. These Old Testament texts point to obedience from the heart as something associated with the coming new covenant. I have focused on the prophets Ezekiel and Jeremiah for several obvious reasons: (1) the new covenant promises in these prophets are clear, and repeated throughout both books, even if they do not generally utilize explicit 'new covenant' language; and (2) New Testament authors cite and allude to both of these prophecies in various ways (we will look at the NT treatment below).

Secondly, I survey key texts in the New Testament which show that the new covenant is a first-century reality, and/or recognize the promise of heart-obedience in the Old Testament and expect the fulfilment of this promise in the new covenant.

Key Old Testament texts: Ezekiel

Ezekiel 36:26–28 points to the new covenant:

> And I will give you a new heart, and a new spirit I will put within you. And I will remove the heart of stone from your flesh and give

you a heart of flesh. And I will put my Spirit within you, and cause you to walk in my statutes and be careful to obey my rules. You shall dwell in the land that I gave to your fathers, and you shall be my people, and I will be your God.

Almost identical language is found in Ezekiel 11:19–20:

And I will give them one heart, and a new spirit I will put within them. I will remove the heart of stone from their flesh and give them a heart of flesh, that they may walk in my statutes and keep my rules and obey them. And they shall be my people, and I will be their God.

Ezekiel 18:31 also echoes these themes:

Cast away from you all the transgressions that you have committed, and make yourselves a new heart and a new spirit! Why will you die, O house of Israel?

Ezekiel 37:14 is similar:

'And I will put my Spirit within you, and you shall live, and I will place you in your own land. Then you will know that I am the LORD; I have spoken, and I will do it,' declares the LORD.

Finally, Ezekiel 39:29:

And I will not hide my face anymore from them, when I pour out my Spirit upon the house of Israel, declares the Lord GOD.

The focus here is on the key themes of Ezekiel 36:26–28. We see these themes repeated often in Ezekiel. The Lord through the prophet Ezekiel is promising a new day, characterized by new hearts, new spirits, the Spirit of God being placed within the covenant people, Spirit-induced or God-caused obedience, true knowledge of God, the people of God truly being 'My people', and God truly being their God. These are promised realities, set in the future. What I will demonstrate below is that if indeed the new covenant has been inaugurated in the ministry of Jesus, then we should expect to see the realities pictured in Ezekiel (and Jeremiah – see below) in new covenant members. Indeed, when we read the New Testament, we find a consistent teaching about the expectation and necessity of heart-obedience to the Lord. It is especially striking when some of the passages above (or at least some of their themes) are picked up by New Testament writers, as they speak of the nature of the Christian life in the new covenant.

Key Old Testament texts: Jeremiah and ancillary passages

The other classic new covenant passage found in the Old Testament is Jeremiah 31:31–34:

> Behold, the days are coming, declares the LORD, when I will make a new covenant with the house of Israel and the house of Judah, not like the covenant that I made with their fathers on the day when I took them by the hand to bring them out of the land of Egypt, my covenant that they broke, though I was their husband, declares the LORD. For this is the covenant that I will make with the house of Israel after those days, declares the LORD: I will put my law within them, and I will write it on their hearts. And I will be their God, and they shall be my people. And no longer shall each one teach his neighbour and each his brother, saying, 'Know the LORD,' for they shall all know me, from the least of them to the greatest, declares the LORD. For I will forgive their iniquity, and I will remember their sin no more.[1]

For my purposes, I will simply note that this new covenant spoken of by the Lord through Jeremiah (1) is not like the Mosaic covenant (v. 32), in that the Mosaic covenant was broken, implying, it seems, that the new covenant will *not* be broken, (2) states that the law will be placed within covenant members and will be written on their hearts, and (3) brings a forgiveness of sins in which God remembers their sins no more – pointing to a fuller and once-for-all forgiveness of sins.

In Jeremiah 4:4, the LORD gives a command to the men of Judah and Jerusalem:

> Circumcise yourselves to the LORD;
> remove the foreskin of your hearts,
> O men of Judah and inhabitants of Jerusalem;

---

[1] Cf. Isa. 54:13: 'All your children shall be taught by the LORD . . .'

> lest my wrath go forth like fire,
> and burn with none to quench it,
> because of the evil of your deeds.

Likewise, Jeremiah 32:40:

> I will make with them an everlasting covenant, that I will not turn away from doing good to them. And I will put the fear of me in their hearts, that they may not turn from me.

Similar to Ezekiel 36:26 and Jeremiah 31:31–34, the Lord is going to put the fear of him in their hearts, so these new covenant members will not turn away.

Likewise, Jeremiah 24:7 reads:

> I will give them a heart to know that I am the LORD, and they shall be my people and I will be their God, for they shall return to me with their whole heart.

According to Jeremiah, God gives his new covenant members hearts to know him, so that these new covenant members will return to the Lord with their whole heart.

Again, Jeremiah 33:8 is similar:

> I will cleanse them from all the guilt of their sin against me, and I will forgive all the guilt of their sin and rebellion against me.

Likewise, Jeremiah 33:14:

> Behold, the days are coming, declares the LORD, when I will fulfil the promise I made to the house of Israel and the house of Judah.

Likewise, Jeremiah 30:22:

> And you shall be my people,
> And I will be your God.

Finally, Jeremiah 50:20:

> In those days and in that time, declares the LORD, iniquity shall be sought in Israel, and there shall be none, and sin in Judah,

and none shall be found, for I will pardon those whom I leave as
a remnant.

Briefly, two texts from Isaiah. First, Isaiah 44:3:

> For I will pour water on the thirsty land,
>   and streams on the dry ground;
> I will pour my Spirit upon your offspring,
>   and my blessing on your descendants.

And secondly, Isaiah 59:21:

> 'And as for me, this is my covenant with them,' says the LORD: 'My
> Spirit that is upon you, and my words that I have put in your
> mouth, shall not depart out of your mouth, or out of the mouth
> of your offspring, or out of the mouth of your children's offspring,'
> says the LORD, 'from this time forth and forevermore'.

Two texts from Proverbs are worthy of note. Proverbs 3:3:

> Let not steadfast love and faithfulness forsake you;
>   bind them around your neck;
>   write them on the tablet of your heart.

And Proverbs 7:3:

> bind them on your fingers;
>   write them on the tablet of your heart.

Both passages are intriguing in that they point to the importance of
God's law being written on the human heart.

Numerous other passages, such as Proverbs 1:23, Isaiah 44:3, 32:15,
11:2, Zechariah 12:10 – 13:1 and Joel 2:28–29 speak of a future where
God's Spirit will be poured out on his people.

But let us return to Jeremiah 31. Here we read of the Lord's promise
through the prophet that he will forgive their iniquity. This should give
us pause, for it appears that the forgiveness of sins is *not* a unique feature
of the new covenant but is simply a key element in both old and new
covenants. But how is forgiveness a *unique* feature of the new covenant?

Here is one way of thinking through this issue: (1) Jeremiah 31:34
promises that the Lord will 'forgive their iniquity' and 'remember their

sin no more, and *since* (2) there certainly *was* forgiveness for Old Testament believers, it may be the case *that* (3) one of the differences between old covenant and new is not simply the *scope* of forgiveness (100 per cent of covenant members are forgiven), but that there is a profounder and *permanent* forgiveness of sins – rooted in the 'better' nature of the new covenant, an improvement that at least includes a more intense pouring out or presence of the Holy Spirit in the lives of new covenant members.

Joshua N. Moon argues for an 'Augustinian' reading of the new covenant (the 'later' Augustine, as Moon sees it; i.e. later in Augustine's theological development). As Moon interprets Augustine, 'the contrast of membership in the old and new covenants is nothing less than the contrast of membership between the city of man and the city of God: unfaithfulness with the law opposed to grace and faith, the work of the Spirit'.[2] According to Moon, Augustine understood the 'new covenant' – particularly the new covenant as summarized and prophesied in Jeremiah 31 – not to be a new state or era in redemptive history, for such a view makes it extremely difficult to account for the saving faith manifested in the Old Testament saints. Rather, the new covenant is simply the condition of all true believers. That is, if you are a true believer in the one true God of holy Scripture – *whether living before or after the death/burial/resurrection of Jesus* – you are part of the *new* covenant. As Moon concludes, 'The characteristics of the members of the "new covenant" in Jeremiah are nothing other than the characteristics of a faithful believer in any era.'[3] Similarly, Moon writes, 'At the heart of an Augustinian reading of Jeremiah's new covenant, as developed in this work, lies the view that Jeremiah 31:31–34 does not contrast two successive eras in redemptive history, but rather two standings before God.'[4]

While I am loathe to disagree with the Doctor of Grace (Augustine) – as interpreted by Moon – I still suspect that it is correct to see a historical-redemptive nature to the biblical covenants. That is, that there is a historical flow to the covenants, and that Moon's construal too easily flattens the covenantal development across the canon. The new covenant has *come* in the ministry of Jesus, and was *promised* and *prophesied* in Jeremiah 31 (cf. Ezek. 36 and ancillary passages). One need not posit a radical law–gospel *contrast* to affirm that there is a historical flow to the covenants and that the new covenant was

[2] Moon 2011: 28.
[3] Ibid. 29.
[4] Ibid. 245.

actually *new* – historically new in a historical-redemptive sense. Indeed, we see in Hebrews 8:13 the following: 'In speaking of a new covenant, he makes the first one obsolete. And what is becoming obsolete and growing old is ready to vanish away.' Note that the old covenant is *becoming* obsolete. Such language seems to presume that there was a historical-redemptive shift in the first century, and that central to this historical-redemptive shift was the emergence or establishing of a *new* covenant.

Similarly, we read in Hebrews 9:1 a description of the 'first' covenant: it had 'regulations for worship', an 'earthly place of holiness', a tent, lampstand, the table, the bread of presence, and so on. But surely such language of the 'first' (old) covenant is not describing a covenant that was simply a covenant of unbelief, or a necessarily 'unfaithful' state before God. Rather, this first (old) covenant was given by God, and was a good covenant, a covenant initiated by the grace of God (Exod. 20:1). And this covenant is becoming obsolete *not* because it was *fundamentally* a covenant of unbelief (as widespread as that was!); otherwise, one is *still* stuck with the conundrum of explaining *belief* or *saving faith* among Old Testament saints. Indeed, Moon's Augustinian reading seems to exacerbate the problem, or at least one of the problems, it is seeking to solve – that is, the nature of saving faith among Old Testament saints. For if true belief in no way relates to the temple, to sacrifices, to God's law, and so on, then the entire Old Testament sacrificial and religious system becomes virtually inexplicable. That is, is a *true* and *saving* relationship with God completely divorced from the entire cultic/religious system God himself prescribed?

One can affirm a historical-redemptive understanding of the covenants, that is, *at least* a partial element of promise–fulfilment, or shadow–reality, unfolding of the covenants over time at play in the Christian canon, but not root this in a radical law–gospel contrast. That is, one can see a good bit of continuity across the canon, but still affirm there is 'newness' to the new covenant whereby the new covenant era is a new era in redemptive history. I mention the law–gospel contrast because it is possible to differ from Moon's 'Augustinian' reading of Jeremiah 31 *without* doing so from the position of a radical law–gospel contrast. That is, one can *affirm* that the law is 'holy and righteous and good' (Rom. 7:12), can affirm that the law *truly ought to have been kept*, and can affirm that even in the new covenant era there is a 'third use' of the law applicable to Christians – as long as, *mutatis mutandis*, we interpret the law in the light of the *historical-redemptive* shift that has taken place through the entrance of Jesus into the world, and in the light of his death, burial and resurrection.

The goal then is to do full justice to (1) the newness of the new covenant, a newness that includes (but is not limited to) an affirmation that the new covenant is a new *era* in the history of redemption, and (2) the place of Spirit-induced and gospel-driven obedience in the Christian life. In both covenants the people of God are expected to obey God's word – including commands, prescriptions, statutes, and so on. The challenge is to do full justice to the place of works, obedience and faithfulness in the new covenant while also doing full justice to the historical-redemptive shift that has occurred. One must not collapse/inflate old and new covenant into one another, nor drive an unbiblical wedge between the covenants, such that it becomes impossible to make sense of the necessity of works, obedience and faithfulness in the new covenant.

But let us return to Jeremiah 31. It appears that one of the factors which make the new covenant *new* is that it entails a profounder forgiveness than that found in the old covenant. In short, I am arguing for a *qualitative* difference between the old and new covenants, not just a *quantitative* difference. Since God did indeed forgive sins committed in the old covenant era, we must ask why a mark of the new covenant is that sins would be forgiven.

Rolf Rendtorff's seminal work *The Covenant Formula* is extremely helpful in coming to terms with the heart of Jeremiah 31. Rendtorff states something that might seem obvious, but can easily be over-looked. In promising a new covenant, the law is not *abolished* but actually *reaffirmed*, although we must also ask how the incarnation, death, burial and resurrection of Jesus shape how we *now* relate to the law. Rendtorff writes, 'Here the text talks about the Torah as the real substance of the covenant – almost in passing, because for this author that was evidently a matter of course.'[5] Hence we cannot forget that in the new covenant it is the *law* that has been placed within the believer. Indeed, Christians must wrestle with the way in which they must relate to the law this side of the death, burial, resurrection and ascension of Jesus. However, since God in the new covenant has placed the law in the hearts of new covenant members, we have at the least prima facie reasons for exploring the place of obedience (or works or faithfulness) in the new covenant.

[5] Rendtorff 1998: 73.

The New Testament and new covenant themes from the Old Testament

It is clear from the New Testament that the life, death, burial and resurrection of Jesus have – at the least – inaugurated the new covenant. We see this in Lord's Supper passages (Luke 22:20; Matt. 26:28; Mark 14:24; 1 Cor. 11:25), as well as other New Testament passages that speak of the New Covenant (2 Cor. 3:6; Heb. 8:8, 13; 9:15; 12:24; cf. Heb. 7:22; 8:6 – 'better' covenant). I turn briefly to these New Testament texts, which allude to Old Testament texts promising the new covenant (particularly in Ezekiel and Jeremiah), the presence of the Spirit or the reality of Spirit-produced/God-wrought obedience.

Hebrews

It is not an overstatement to say that the central point of Hebrews is the superior nature of the new covenant in comparison to the old covenant. O'Brien writes on the use of Jeremiah 31 in Hebrews 8, 'To know God is to recognize him, to trust him, to obey him.'[6] He rightly notes that a number of *similarities* and *commonalities* between the old and new covenant are highlighted in Hebrews:

- Both are based on divine promises (8:6).
- Both have the same goal: 'I will be their God, / and they will be my people' (8:10).
- Both were lawfully established (7:11; 8:6).
- Both include laws (7:5, 16, 28; 8:10).
- Both provide for the forgiveness of sins (8:12).

So what is the key difference? As O'Brien sees it, 'the new covenant is established on *better promises*'.[7] That is, God gives new hearts to new covenant believers, 'so ensuring obedience to his will'.[8]

The 'better' nature of the new covenant is emphasized throughout Hebrews 9 and 10. The system of the first covenant (9:1–10) is contrasted with Christ's priestly work in the better covenant (9:11–14). The new covenant has a 'greater and more perfect tent' (9:11). Jesus enters 'once for all' with his own blood, not that of goats and calves (9:12–13). Jesus' death – he is a better priest offering a better sacrifice

---

[6] O'Brien 2010: 300.
[7] Ibid. 301; emphasis original.
[8] Ibid.

– provides forgiveness for sins committed under the prior covenantal epoch, the old covenant: 'a death has occurred that redeems them from the transgressions committed under the first covenant' (9:15). As O'Brien notes, 'His [Jesus'] redemptive sacrifice is retrospective in its effects and is valid for all who trusted God for the forgiveness of sins in ancient Israel (11:40).'[9] Jesus is mediator of the new covenant *so that* 'those who are called may receive the promised eternal inheritance'. That is, in order for God's promise of an eternal inheritance to come to fulfilment, it was necessary (cf. 9:23) that Jesus mediate a new covenant. For the author of Hebrews this new covenant has clearly been inaugurated in the ministry of Jesus.

As Hebrews proceeds to argue, the tabernacle/temple was a type of 'copy' of the heavenly realities (the heavenly sanctuary). And the sacrificial rites of the Old Testament were necessary to purify these copies. But now the heavenly realities *themselves* need to be purified (9:23–26), and it is for this purifying purpose that Christ offered himself. Hebrews 10 carries forward the argument, emphasizing the 'once for all' (10:10) nature of Christ's sacrifice. Obviously, the book of Hebrews assumes (and explicates) that the new covenant is a true reality from the first century onwards.

The Lord's Supper in the New Testament

All three Synoptic Gospels feature the Lord's Supper, and identify it as a new covenant reality. Matthew and Mark both speak of the cup as 'my blood of the covenant' (Matt. 26:28; Mark 14:24). Luke 22:20 speaks of the 'cup that is poured out for you' as 'the new covenant in my blood'. When Paul speaks of the Lord's Supper in 1 Corinthians 11:20–33, he writes, 'In the same way also he took the cup, after supper, saying, "This cup is the new covenant in my blood"' (v. 25). Apparently, neither Jesus nor Paul feels the need to argue for the reality of the new covenant. In the Synoptic Gospels, both the death of Christ and the meal that precedes his death are clearly presented in terms of a new covenant. Paul claims to have received his understanding or teaching of the Lord's Supper 'from the Lord' (11:23), and understands the death of Christ to be a marker or indicator of the new covenant. In short, in the Synoptic Gospels and in Paul's teaching in 1 Corinthians, the new covenant is seen as a present reality in the first century.

[9] Ibid. 328.

2 Corinthians 3

This is the most significant passage where the themes from Ezekiel and Jeremiah are picked up, as noted particularly by Scott Hafemann.[10] I will not attempt to navigate whether any of the Old Testament texts was more dominant in Paul's own thought. All of the following have been suggested by different scholars as possible background to Paul's teaching here. Referring to stone tablets: Exodus 24:12; 31:18; 32:15; 34:1; Deuteronomy 9:10. Referring to new hearts or the presence of Spirit: Jeremiah 31:33; Ezekiel 11:19; 36:26–28; Proverbs 3:3; 7:3.[11] For my purposes here, I will assume it is clear that these presence of the Spirit passages influenced Paul, and form the background for his teaching in 2 Corinthians 3.[12] In 2 Corinthians 3:3–18, Paul's teaching is that the eschatological (or new covenant) age prophesied in Ezekiel (11:19; 36:26–27; cf. 18:31; 37:14; 39:29) and the new covenant prophesied in Jeremiah 31:33–34 have broken into history. Paul clearly speaks of the 'new covenant' (*kainēs diathēkēs*; 2 Cor. 3:6). He also emphasizes that the recipients are his 'letter', and this letter is 'written in our hearts' (v. 2; cf. Ezek. 11:19–20; 36:26–28; Jer. 31:31–34). This letter is 'written not with ink but with the Spirit of the living God, not on tablets of stone but on tablets of human hearts' (v. 3; cf. Ezek. 11:19–20; 36:26–28; Jer. 31:31–34). Paul writes of God, 'who has made us sufficient to be ministers of a new covenant, not of the letter but of the Spirit. For the letter kills, but the Spirit gives life' (2 Cor. 3:6; cf. Ezek. 11:19–20; 36:26–28; Jer. 31:31–34). So Paul Barnett comments on 2 Corinthians 3, 'The Law of God has been internalized in hearts made alive by the Spirit of the living God (see Jer. 31:33; cf. v. 6).'[13]

Romans 2:25–29

Romans 2:25–29 is an important passage because Paul explicitly links circumcision, obedience to the law, and the Holy Spirit. Paul argues that it is the one who keeps God's precepts who is truly circumcised (vv. 25–26). Indeed, the true Jew is the one who has a 'matter of the heart' circumcision, which has been brought about by the Spirit of God. Although Paul does not use *exact* phrases from Jeremiah and

[10] Cf. Hafemann on 2 Cor. 3: 1990; 1995; 2000.
[11] Cf. Hafemann 1990: 209–220.
[12] Ibid. 211. Hafemann notes that C. Wolff finds Prov. 3:3 and 7:3 to be determinative here: 'the determination of allusions is by no means easily carried out, especially when biblical terminology has become an essential part of an author's own vocabulary, as it certainly has with Paul'.
[13] Barnett 1997: 169.

Ezekiel, he is most certainly in the same *conceptual* world as the key passages we have looked at from those two prophets. When Paul speaks of an inward circumcision of the heart (2:28–29) linked with obedience from the heart, we are in the conceptual world of the weeping prophet and of Ezekiel. It is appropriate to glance forward to the end of Romans 3, where Paul explicitly raises a potential misunderstanding of his teaching: does faith 'overthrow' the law? Certainly not! Rather, Paul writes, 'we uphold the law' (3:31). Paul mitigates the 'hard' contrast with 3:27 ('By what kind of law? By a law of works? No, but by the law of faith') by his statement in 3:31 that he is attempting to *uphold* the law. One of God's key goals has *always* been obedience from the heart, and this prophesied and promised state of affairs is now coming true in the first century. Thus, central to the life of the new covenant member there are – in Paul's mind – three linked realities: spiritual circumcision, obedience to God's precepts, the Holy Spirit. It is the Spirit who truly circumcises, and when the Spirit circumcises, the result is obedience to God's precepts.

1 Thesssalonians 4:8

In 1 Thesssalonians 4:8, Paul speaks of 'God, who gives His Holy Spirit to you'. David Peterson suggests that Paul is here recalling Ezekiel 36:27, which reads, 'And I will put my Spirit within you, and cause you to walk in my statutes and be careful to obey my rules.'[14] Certainly, Paul seems to have the new covenant in mind in the very next verse, 1 Thessalonians 4:9: 'Now concerning brotherly love you have no need for anyone to write to you, for you yourselves have been taught by God to love one another,' recalling Jeremiah 31:34, where the Lord through the prophet says, 'And no longer shall each one teach his neighbour and each his brother, saying, "Know the LORD," for they shall all know me.' Paul is recalling Ezekiel 36:26–28 and Jeremiah 31, and understands the state of affairs portrayed in these prophetic texts as being fulfilled in the first century.

Other New Testament passages

A number of New Testament passages state Christians no longer have need of anyone to teach them, for they all know God (or variations on this theme). This clearly reflects the teaching of Jeremiah 31. For example, in John 6:45, Jesus teaches, 'It is written in the prophets, "AND THEY SHALL ALL BE TAUGHT OF GOD." Everyone who has heard

---

[14] Peterson 1995: 84.

and learned from the Father, comes to me' (NASB). 1 John 2:27 is particularly interesting: 'But the anointing that you received from him abides in you, and you have no need that anyone should teach you. But as his anointing teaches you about everything, and is true, and is no lie – just as it has taught you, abide in him.'

Note that following 'have no need that anyone should teach you' John notes, 'abide in Him'.[15] While John does not expound on this in detail, texts of this kind denote that the new covenant reality of not needing to be taught is linked to our relationship with Christ – that is, since in the new covenant there is a relationship with Christ that surpasses anything found in the old covenant.[16]

Similarly, in 2 Corinthians 1:21 Paul links being in Christ with anointing: 'And it is God who establishes us with you in Christ, and has anointed us.' In Ephesians 6:6, Paul admonishes slaves/servants to obey their master as they would obey Christ. This should be a true obedience 'from the heart', analogous to obeying Christ. By obeying their masters, they do the 'will of God from the heart'.

Interestingly, in Acts 10:38 Jesus' being anointed with the Holy Spirit is linked with Jesus' own good deeds and healings: 'God anointed Jesus of Nazareth with the Holy Spirit and with power. He went about doing good and healing all who were oppressed by the devil, for God was with him.' Such a passage is significant for a fortiori reasons: if Jesus' own good deeds and healings are somehow linked to (dependent upon?) the anointing of the Holy Spirit, how much more are *our* actions linked to (and certainly dependent upon) the Holy Spirit?

Likewise, John 3:2 reads, 'This man came to Jesus by night and said to him, "Rabbi, we know that you are a teacher come from God, for no one can do these signs that you do unless God is with him."' In Nicodemus' encounter with Jesus, Nicodemus testifies to the link between Jesus' coming from God and the signs that Jesus has performed (John 3:2).[17]

[15] Whether the verb 'abide' (*menete*) is taken as an imperative (a command) or an indicative (stating what is already in fact the case), my point remains: there is a link between abiding in Christ and not having need of anyone to teach the believer.

[16] Commentators do not tend to see texts like Jer. 31 and Ezek. 36 (and ancillary texts) in the background here (so Bruce, Kruse, Schnackenberg and Smalley). Nonetheless, since not needing 'anyone to teach you' is conceptually in full accord with such OT texts, it seems plausible that 1 John 2:27 can be read against such texts. Carson 2004 notes this connection.

[17] John 3:2 reads, 'this man came to Jesus by night and said to Him, "Rabbi, we know that You have come from God *as* a teacher; for no one can do these signs that You do unless God is with him"' (NASB).

Conclusion

In this chapter I have attempted to lay out a basic biblical backdrop against which one might make sense of the importance of works, obedience and faithfulness. I began by noting that in two key Old Testament prophetic books – Jeremiah and Ezekiel (and ancillary passages) – there is a pattern in which a future day is coming, a day that will see Spirit-induced, God-caused obedience from the heart. This is pictured in different ways in different passages, but the pattern is clear, and one of the central marks of this approaching era is heart-obedience, an obedience ultimately elicited by God. I then turned to two New Testament themes. First, there is affirmation that the new covenant has entered into history through the ministry of Jesus. Secondly, there is also affirmation that the writers saw the key themes from Jeremiah and Ezekiel as realities in the first century.

Before going further, it is necessary to question how we think about the continuities and discontinuities across the canon. Arguably, this is the sine qua non of biblical theology: coming to terms with these as we work through the historical-redemptive nature of holy writ. To some of these fundamental issues we now turn.

Chapter Three

Old covenant, new covenant and the history of redemption

This chapter will explore a few hermeneutical issues concerning the relationship between the old and new covenants, especially the unity and coherence of the Scriptures – with a focus on the role of works, obedience and faithfulness. I will argue that works, obedience and faithfulness are essential aspects of the believer's life throughout the canon. The question of continuity and discontinuity in Scripture is of course a significant one, and this chapter will deal with issues that arise from that question. I will argue that throughout Scripture works, obedience and faithfulness are constitutive elements of the believer's life.

Continuity and discontinuity: getting the question right

When one begins to read the Bible seriously, one key issue that emerges is the question of the relation between the covenants. Does the new covenant *replace* the old covenant? Does the new covenant *fulfil* the old covenant – and what exactly does that mean? *Restate* or *reaffirm* – *à la* theonomy? *Exist alongside of* – as in some sort of 'two-track' path (Jewish and Christian) to God? One hermeneutical dyad is to choose between two competing paradigms: either (1) one should *presume continuity* – any and every old covenant teaching or prescription or command is binding unless rejected or abrogated in the new covenant; or (2) one should *presume discontinuity* – any and every old covenant teaching or prescription or command has been abrogated unless reaffirmed in the new covenant. Some forms of covenant theology adopt the 'presume continuity' option, while some forms of dispensationalism adopt the 'presume discontinuity' position. It is easy to believe that one must choose between these two.

To get caught up into these two options as the only viable paths is to miss the historical-redemptive nature of the canon, and to misunderstand the new covenant as the 'next stage' of God's plan. Rather, since the death, burial and resurrection of Jesus is the linchpin of the history of redemption (indeed, of all history), we should be open to seeing the new covenant's relation to the old covenant in more dynamic ways than simply 'continuity' or 'discontinuity'.

Hafemann suggests that as we move from old covenant to new, there is a significant shift in redemptive history.[1] Only *some persons* in the old covenant had the Holy Spirit (i.e. persons could be 'in' the covenant but not be changed or transformed by the Holy Spirit), while *all persons* in the new covenant have the Holy Spirit. This is fundamentally correct. However, it is less certain that the 'newness' of the new covenant denotes no difference in the *kind* or *intensity* of the work of the Holy Spirit. To clarify: Hafemann affirms that the new covenant is *quantitatively* better, but does not say the new covenant is *qualitatively* better. To return to a key text from the last chapter, Jeremiah 31:34, in speaking of the new covenant, reads, 'For I will forgive their iniquity, and I will remember their sin no more.' This is a puzzling passage, for at least two interlocking reasons: (1) the old covenant and the new covenant are *contrasted*; (2) one of the realities of the new covenant is the forgiveness of sins, *but there was already forgiveness of sins in the old covenant* (Lev. 4:26, 31, 35; 5:10, 13, 16, 18; 6:7; 19:22; Num. 14:19; 15:25–26, 28).[2]

So, if there is forgiveness in both the old and new covenants, why is one of the *marks* of the new covenant that 'I will forgive their iniquity, and I will remember their sin no more'? If Hafemann is correct, the key difference is one of scope: *all covenant members* in the new covenant will have circumcised hearts and will be forgiven, while *some covenant members* in the old covenant had circumcised hearts and were truly forgiven. In short, for Hafemann the key difference between old and new covenants – in terms of forgiveness – is one of *scope*: *some* covenant members during the old covenant era are truly forgiven, while *all* covenant members during the new covenant era are forgiven (i.e. the new covenant is *quantitatively* better).

This *some forgiven* versus *all forgiven* dynamic is certainly true – at least a part of the truth. But if this is all we say about the 'newness'

---

[1] For a particularly helpful summary of his thinking on *covenant*, see Hafemann 2007.

[2] As noted earlier, Moon 2011 argues for an 'Augustinian' reading of Jer. 31:31–34. Moon's thesis, as summarized in the last chapter, is as follows: 'Rather than seeing the contrast to be one of degree, quality, or development (such as a contrast within redemptive-history, from Old Testament to New Testament eras), Augustinian readings see the contrast as absolute: a contrast between apostasy or infidelity and faithfulness, or two mutually exclusive ways of standing before God' (2011: 3).

of the new covenant, we are going to miss something. There is some sort of historical-redemptive shift as we move from old covenant to new, whereby the 'newness' of the new covenant consists not only in a shift in the scope of the new covenant (a quantitative change), but there is also a shift in the kind of pouring out of the Holy Spirit (a qualitative change). Thus, as one moves from old covenant to new, there is not simply (1) a quantitative difference – a greater percentage of the covenant people possessing the Holy Spirit and possessing forgiveness, but also (2) a qualitative difference – a more intense presence of the Holy Spirit.[3] Calvin affirms this: the Holy Spirit was given to Old Testament believers, 'but that it was not yet so bright and illustrious as it would afterwards become'.[4]

Henri Blocher on old and new covenant

I find it hard to improve upon the summary of Henri Blocher on the question of the old and new covenant. Blocher, while affirming an overarching and real theological unity to the Christian canon, contends that the student of Scripture must also come to terms with the discontinuities between the old and new covenant. In examining Blocher's understanding of the relationship between the old and new covenant, we should note his summary of the relationship of God to man in the garden. He writes, 'the benefits of the Eden covenant are purely gratuitous; the condition (unfailing ratification of one's image-creature dependence on God) is nothing else than continuation in grace'.[5] Blocher can speak of the reality of human obedience without falling into 'legalism' (as this book will argue):

> It must be noted, however, that the legal principle, 'He who does these things shall live in them' and 'He who does not shall die' is strictly in force. This is no legalism! Life is no reward given after works have been done; it is first a gift of grace. Yet, it is responsibility. The creational covenant establishes the regime of human responsibility *coram Deo* (before God).[6]

---

[3] Hamilton 2006 lays out six positions concerning whether old covenant members were individually indwelt by the Holy Spirit, and the related question of the continuity between old covenant and new. See esp. ch. 2.

[4] Calvin 1979: 310; quoted in Hamilton 2006: 14.

[5] Blocher 2006: 258.

[6] Ibid.

Blocher is tapping into the proper historical-redemptive trajectory when he writes, '*Since the covenant of grace is founded on a precise historical event (the cross of Calvary), since it is concluded in Jesus Christ the incarnate Son, believers in previous ages could share in its benefits only proleptically.*'[7] And Blocher quotes O. Palmer Robertson approvingly: 'Only in anticipation of the finished work of Christ could an act of heart-renewal be performed under the provisions of the old covenant.'[8] Perhaps now we are able to make sense of the Lord's promise to Jeremiah (31:34), for 'I will forgive their iniquity, and I will remember their sin no more'. In short, my suggestion is that there is a profounder forgiveness of sins in the new covenant. The forgiveness of sins in the old covenant (Lev. 4:26, 31, 35; 5:10, 16; 6:7) was (1) real, (2) proleptically related to the death, burial, resurrection, ascension and intercession of Christ, and (3) in some mysterious sense less than fully realized by Old Testament saints. It is worth quoting Blocher at length. The biblical writers

> represent sins that God had forgiven under the Old Testament, but which had not been objectively done away with by the sacrifice of goats and bulls, as 'stored' somewhere and waiting for the true atonement to be made: Hebrews 9:15, Romans 3:25 (*paresis*, God had left them unpunished, in an apparent denial of his justice). With such a sense of successive time, the proleptic character of the experience of grace before the coming of Christ called for a concrete marking. Enjoyment in advance could not be full and free, as full and free as it is in the Christian era.[9]

At the end of his essay 'Old Covenant, New Covenant' Blocher deals briefly with the question of obedience within the 'covenant of grace'. Even if one does not want to use the traditional 'covenant of grace' nomenclature, Blocher's description of works and obedience within a fundamentally gracious relationship is helpful. Blocher writes, 'The repetition of the principle of legal responsibility, which, in Eden,

---

[7] Ibid. 260; emphasis original. Note well, while Blocher uses the phrase 'covenant of grace', he is not – ultimately – working with a 'covenant of works'/'covenant of grace' scheme, at least in how this scheme tends to be understood. This will become clear throughout my treatment of Blocher.

[8] Robertson 1980: 292. Robertson is relying on Calvin, as Blocher notes. Robertson quotes from Calvin on Jeremiah: 'the power, then, to penetrate into the heart was not inherent in the law, but it was a benefit transferred to the law from the gospel'. Cf. Blocher 2006: 260.

[9] Blocher 2006: 260–262.

was the formula of life enduring in fellowship with God and, after sin, becomes that of inescapable condemnation, is only one element in the complexity of the Sinaitic arrangement.'[10] Thus it seems that for Blocher 'the principle of legal responsibility' is neither inherently nor fundamentally a 'works-principle' nor (necessarily) a 'covenant of works' or a so-called 'republication' of a covenant of works. But after sin such a 'principle of legal responsibility' becomes in fact a pointer to inescapable condemnation. Thus (1) in man's pre-fall state (where Blocher can say there is already grace, contra scholars like Kline), God gives commands that are meant to be obeyed and, since man is not yet in bondage to sin, truly can be obeyed; (2) in man's post-fall state God gives commands, and these commands are intrinsically good, righteous and holy (Rom. 7:7, 12), these commands ought to be obeyed. For both Old and New Testament saints alike there is some real ability, due to the reality of circumcised hearts and the presence of the Spirit, to obey really, but not yet perfectly.[11]

There is a real spiritual power for obedience in both the old covenant and the new. Believers in both covenants have a power to obey – a power dependent on having circumcised hearts and the presence of the Spirit. Indeed, there is not only a quantitative difference between the covenants (i.e. in the new covenant all covenant members have circumcised hearts, or are regenerate, while in the old covenant only some covenant members have circumcised hearts, or are regenerate), but also a qualitative difference (i.e. there is a profounder pouring out or presence of the Spirit in the new covenant).[12] However, it is critical to make the theological link between the person and work of Christ and the forgiveness available to saints in the Old Testament period. That is, if we affirm an atoning power to forgive in the Old Testament era, but then fail to affirm the proleptic and forward-looking nature of the sacrificial system of the Old Testament (i.e. the way the sacrifices participated in, or looked forward to, the sacrifice of Christ), we risk grounding the forgiveness of sins in different realities as we move from old to new covenant. We will also miss the uniqueness of the new covenant, and that the ministry of Jesus (including his death, burial and resurrection) was the goal of the law and promises (Rom. 10:4; Luke 24:27, 45–47; John 5:46).

---

[10] Ibid. 268.

[11] Note, I am not addressing all issues related to the nature of the Spirit's work in the old and new covenant. See Hamilton 2006 and Block 1989.

[12] Blocher speaks of '*a change of "level"*': 'The level of the operations of the covenant of grace is, emphatically, inward and spiritual' (2006: 269; emphasis original).

Law and gospel, gospel and law: the nature of the new covenant and the question of salvation of Old Testament saints

One of the key questions that emerges as we wrestle with the nature of the new covenant concerns the relationship of law and gospel. This has become an important issue in contemporary Protestant theology, but here is not the place to deal with it. Nonetheless, the question cannot be avoided, for in taking up the issue of works, obedience and faithfulness, always lurking in the background is the question of law and gospel. Some have posited a strong law–gospel contrast, suggesting that an antithesis of law and gospel lies at the heart of understanding the message of the Bible. If indeed the Bible is structured by a strong law–gospel antithesis, it is understandable that there will be (if even unnecessarily so) a strong antithesis between faith and works, or between grace and human agency (works, obedience or faithfulness) of virtually any kind. And then, at least for Protestants, we are back to Berkouwer's important question, quoted at the beginning of this monograph, about justification by faith alone making all further discussion (regarding works) 'superfluous'.[13] That is, if the law–gospel relationship is seen as a radical antithesis, it is understandable that one would be inclined to see a radical antithesis between grace and works, faith and works, and so on (even if, technically, such a radical antithesis between grace and works, faith and works was not necessary).

A radical law–gospel antithesis is commonly attributed to Martin Luther and Lutheran orthodoxy. It is also suggested that traditional Reformed theology or Reformed orthodoxy has a more modified understanding of the purported law–gospel contrast or antithesis. However, this scenario is not so neat and clean. First, some of the strongest calls for a strong law–gospel contrast are coming from certain *Reformed* circles. Thus the faculty at Westminster Seminary California appears to see such a law–gospel antithesis as essential, and as central to the Reformed tradition.[14] Secondly, there is a lively discussion

[13] Berkouwer 1952: 17.

[14] See Clark 2007. Cf. the response to that book: Sandlin 2007. One particularly prominent advocate of a strong law–gospel contrast or distinction is Michael Horton. Horton stresses a law–gospel antithesis, *but only at the point of justification*: 'Even the law that accused us now appears to us as a delight. Luther writes: the law "no longer terrifies us with death and hell but has become our kind friend and companion." Christ has turned the prison into a palace. "He did not destroy and abrogate the Law; but He

among traditional Lutherans, with some suggesting that Luther himself (and significant portions of the Lutheran tradition following him) was quite open to, and even affirming of, a 'third use' of the law.[15] Thus, while the Lutheran theologian Edward A. Engelbrecht continues to affirm the 'law and gospel dialectic', he argues that Luther, Melanchthon and the Formula of Concord are all fundamentally in agreement in affirming a 'third use' of the law for Christians.[16]

Law and gospel: friend or foe?

A lot hinges on how one understands continuity and discontinuity across the canon. I will allow John Frame to set the stage for exploring this seminal question. Frame has authored an especially helpful essay, 'Law and Gospel'.[17] While faith receives what Christ has done, Frame notes that faith is also commanded by God, and thus 'is like other divine commands'.[18] Frame notes, 'So it is impossible to say that command, or law, is excluded from the message of the gospel.'[19] Frame is self-consciously and intentionally distancing himself from a thoroughgoing law–gospel contrast. Thus, he writes, having just turned to Isaiah 52:7, 'So the gospel includes law in an important sense: God's kingdom authority, his demand to repent. Even in the view of those most committed to the law/gospel distinction, the gospel includes a command to *believe*.'[20]

Frame suggests that the gospel really comes *first* in God's dealings with man. He continues, 'That is the pattern of the Decalogue, as we

so changed our heart . . . and made the Law so lovely to it that the heart so delights and rejoices in nothing more than the Law. It would not willingly see one tittle of it fall away." Thus even the law depends on the gospel for its efficacy. The distinction between law and gospel, works and faith, and the covenant of works and covenant of grace does not, at least in Reformed theology, imply an absolute antithesis except at the point of how one is accepted by God. To distinguish the respective nature and role of command and promise is not to denigrate, much less repudiate, either. . . . Yet God's gift of new obedience can in no way serve as a second instrument of justification, nor can faith be defined as obedience (faith formed by love) in the act of justifying sinners. Certainly not at every point, but *where justification is concerned,* faith and works are absolutely antithetical (Rom 3:20–28; 4:4–5, 13–17; 10:1–13; 11:6; Gal 2:16–21; 3:2–14, 21–4:31; Eph 2:8–9; 2 Tim 1:9)' (2007: 217–218; emphasis original).

[15] See Engelbrecht 2011 and S. R. Murray 2002. The entire July–October 2005 issue of *Concordia Theological Quarterly* was devoted to the question of the use of the law in Lutheran theology.

[16] Engelbrecht 2011: 252–253.

[17] Frame 2002.

[18] Ibid. 3.

[19] Ibid.

[20] Ibid.

have seen: God proclaims that he has redeemed his people (gospel), then asks them to behave as his covenant people (law). Since both gospel and law are aspects of God's covenants, that pattern pervades Scripture.'[21]

Frame also raises a concern central to the argument of this monograph: certain understandings of salvation, and of justification in particular, can, if one is not careful, lead to an unbiblical passivity. Thus it would appear that some, with a commendable passion to guard the objective nature of justification (i.e. Christ has done, outside us, what is necessary for our justification), are unable to speak meaningfully about the subjective change wrought in the believer. Thus, as Frame notes:

> This understanding [which is zealous to guard the objective nature of justification] focuses on justification: God regards us as objectively righteous for Christ's sake, apart from anything in us. But it tends to neglect regeneration and sanctification: that God does work real subjective changes in the justified.[22]

In a lengthy review of Meredith Kline's *Kingdom Prologue: Genesis Foundations for a Covenantal Worldview*, Frame makes a number of helpful criticisms. While there is much in Kline that I would affirm, it is helpful to contrast what both Frame and Kline say about the obedience of persons – particularly under the Abrahamic and Mosaic covenants. Kline was a careful expositor of Scripture, so he clearly saw that all sorts of 'conditions' were given to God's people, conditions stipulating the necessity of works, obedience and faithfulness. Thus when we turn to the Abrahamic covenant, Kline must reckon with the repeated 'conditions' that must be met in order for Abraham and his seed to receive continued covenantal blessings. To clarify: obedience is somehow necessary for God to pour out his covenantal blessings on Abraham and his seed (see esp. Gen. 18:19; 22:15–18; 26:4–5).

Kline writes that

> a conditionality of human responsibility necessarily entered into the stipulated terms of the covenant of promise. This conditionality did not negate the guarantee of kingdom fulfilment nor did

---

[21] Ibid. 3–4.
[22] Ibid. 4.

the obligations enjoined contradict the pure gospel principle of grace that governed the bestowal of the eternal redemptive blessings.[23]

This is all well and good: one can have grace and conditionality. Indeed, as Kline writes, 'the divine promises of the covenant never existed apart from human obligations'.[24] This, indeed, is a central burden of my own argument. Kline continues, in treating Abraham's obedience, to argue for the 'indispensability of obedience'.[25] Kline works from a strong 'covenant of works' versus 'covenant of grace' distinction, so he explains this clear conditionality in an interesting way. He avers that such 'indispensability of obedience did not, however, amount to the works principle'.[26] According to Kline, we are saved by a 'works principle' (Jesus working on our behalf). Since the work of Abraham (or of us, eventually) must be kept separate from any 'works principle', then Christ's work must be kept separate from Abraham's (or our) work. Hence Abraham's (or our) works/obedience must be kept completely and utterly sequestered from any meaningful connection to our salvation whatsoever. Kline speaks of the real and necessary relationship between Abraham's obedience and the granting of God's covenantal blessings. He writes:

Here the significance of Abraham's works cannot be limited to their role in validation of his own faith. His faithful performance of his covenantal duty is here clearly declared to sustain a causal relationship to the blessing of Isaac and Israel. It had a meritorious character that procured a reward enjoyed by others.[27]

What is Kline saying that differs from the thesis of this book? Namely this: Kline sees that Genesis is full of 'conditions' related to the ultimate fulfilment of the Abrahamic covenant. Abraham's obedience is the 'condition' for God's continuing to grant the covenantal blessings and promises outlined in the Abrahamic covenant (and, for our purposes, we can simply affirm that Gen. 12, 15, 17 and 22 are all components of the God–Abraham relationship).[28] Kline posits a

[23] Kline 2006: 309; quoted in Frame 2011: 177–178.
[24] Kline 2006: 309.
[25] Ibid. 319.
[26] Ibid.
[27] Ibid. 324–325.
[28] For a helpful summary of these various components of the Abrahamic Covenant, see Alexander 1994.

thoroughgoing distinction between (1) earthly/temporal covenantal blessings – having to do with Israel's inheritance of the land of Canaan, and (2) spiritual/heavenly blessings of Abraham's personal salvation and Abraham's descendants in Christ. As Kline writes, 'Though not the ground of the inheritance of heaven, Abraham's obedience was the ground for Israel's inheritance of Canaan. Salvation would not come because of Abraham's obedience, but because of Abraham's obedience salvation would come of the Abrahamites, the Jews (John 4:22).[29]

I both agree and disagree with Kline. He is right to affirm the essential conditionality of the Abrahamic covenant. But he imports unnecessary and unbiblical categories when he posits a strict temporal/earthly versus heavenly/eternal dichotomy, and then says that there are conditions (hence the necessity of obedience) related to the temporal/earthly realm (the realm where a 'works principle' is in play), but there are no conditions (hence not a necessity of obedience) related to the heavenly/spiritual realm (the realm where a 'grace principle' is in play). Does it not make more sense biblically simply to say, God saves people by grace, and within a gracious covenantal relationship expects his people to obey him, and indeed efficaciously moves his covenant people to obey him (cf. Phil. 2:12–13)? And here I am in more agreement with Frame than with Kline. Frame writes of the new covenant believer:

> Today we receive salvation by faith alone, apart from works. But that faith must be a living, working faith, if it is true faith (Jam. 2:14–26). As with Abraham, God rewards our trust, even in the midst of persecution and difficulty (Mk. 10:29–30). Those rewards are the beginning of the rewards we finally inherit at the consummation of God's kingdom.[30]

Frame writes similarly in summarizing his perspective on the Mosaic covenant, again by way of criticizing Kline:

> Since God has redeemed them [the Israelites] by his grace and chosen them by his love, they ought to obey his commandments. . . . But there is nothing substantively different from the pattern of the new covenant. That covenant too is established by God's grace.

---

[29] Kline 2006: 325.
[30] Frame 2011: 181.

But believers, through baptism and public profession (Rom. 10:9–10), promise to follow Christ as Lord.[31]

That is, Frame argues, as I am arguing, that across the canon God saves a people by his grace. Then, *once persons are in covenant relationship with the Lord*, he *then* gives his people commands, statutes, laws, and so on. And he expects his people to obey what he communicates to them.

Insights from Richard Gaffin

Richard Gaffin writes, 'faith and good works, thus distinguished, are always synecdochic. To speak of the one invariably has the other in view; they are unintelligible apart from each other. They always exist without confusion, yet inseparably.'[32] Gaffin's following words are provocative. He contends that the 'law–gospel' antithesis is real, but is simply a part of reality after the fall, and that one of the things the gospel does is to undo this antithesis:

> From this perspective, the antithesis between law and gospel is not an end itself. It is not a theological ultimate. Rather, that antithesis enters not by virtue of creation but as the consequence of sin, and the gospel functions for its overcoming. The gospel is to the end of removing an absolute law–gospel antithesis in the life of the believer. How so? Briefly, apart from the gospel and outside of Christ the law is my enemy and condemns me. Why? Because *God* is my enemy and condemns me. But with the gospel and in Christ, united to him by faith, the law is no longer my enemy but my friend. Why? Because now *God* is no longer my enemy but my friend, and the law, *his* will, the law in its moral core, as reflective of his character and of concerns eternally inherent in his own person and so of what pleases him, is now my friendly guide for life in fellowship with God.[33]

Gaffin links faith, union with Christ and continued obedience: 'The faith by which sinners are justified, as it unites them to Christ and so secures for them all the benefits of salvation there are in him, that

---

[31] Ibid. 186.
[32] Gaffin 2006: 103.
[33] Ibid. 103; emphases original.

faith perseveres to the end and in persevering is never alone.'[34] Gaffin, in the same work, also writes, 'a faith that rests in God the Savior is a faith that is restless to do his will'.[35] Some of these fundamental insights from Gaffin will be worked out in more detail in chapter 5, which focuses on union with Christ.

Geerhardus Vos on law and grace

Some might say that Geerhardus Vos is the grandfather of the contemporary renaissance of biblical theology among evangelicals. His shadow looms large over the world of contemporary evangelical biblical scholarship. Vos nicely summarizes the overarching thesis of this present book:

> It is plain, then, that law-keeping did not figure at that juncture [the Mosaic covenant] as the meritorious ground of life-inheritance. The latter [life-inheritance] is based on grace alone, no less emphatically than Paul himself places salvation on that ground. But, while this is so, it might still be objected that law-observance, if not the ground for receiving, is yet made the ground for retention of the privileges inherited. Here it cannot, of course, be denied that a real connection exists. But the Judaizers went wrong in inferring that the connection must be *meritorious*, that, if Israel keeps the cherished gifts of Jehovah through obedience of His law, this must be so, because in strict justice they had earned them. The connection is of a totally different kind. It belongs not to the legal sphere of merit, but to the symbolico-typical sphere of *appropriateness of expression.*[36]

A little later in the same section of *Biblical Theology* Vos writes, 'law-observance is not the meritorious ground of blessedness'.[37] For a number of reasons this is a fascinating quote. Vos is one of the key proponents of traditional, Reformed, biblical theology. At the same time, Vos – with John Murray, John Frame, and others – denies that a 'works-principle' lies at the heart of the Mosaic covenant. Was Vos flirting with the 'new perspective', before it was even invented? That is, according to Vos, did the Mosaic administration teach that we get

---

[34] Ibid. 105.
[35] Ibid. 78.
[36] Vos 1954: 127; quoted in Frame 2008: 207; emphases original.
[37] Vos 1954: 128.

in by grace and stay in by works? Vos's answer to the question 'Did Israel retain via works or obedience what they had initially received by grace' is 'yes' (properly understood). Vos suggests that Israel did not obtain 'retention of the privileges inherited' because of meritorious works. Nonetheless, there is a *'real connection'* (Vos's words) between 'retention of the privileges inherited' by grace and 'law-observance'. So, what is the nature of the relationship between retaining of privileges and law-observance? For Vos, 'law-observance' does not belong to the 'legal sphere' (which would include or entail the notion of 'merit'), but to the 'symbolico-typical sphere of *appropriateness of expression'*.[38] This is a fascinating move by Vos. Yes, 'law-observance' is essential, but not in a 'meritorious' sense. Rather, 'law-observance' exhibits an 'appropriateness of expression'. I take this to mean that 'law-observance' is not necessary in the sense that we merit something before God, but of course it is necessary and appropriate for those whom God has rescued by grace to obey him, including obedience that consists of 'law-observance'. And thus we return to a central theme of this book: God is rescuing and transforming a people who will love, glorify and serve him from the heart. Works, obedience and faithfulness are 'necessary' in that such realities are simply *constitutive of a redeemed life.* And such a life flows from a heart radically transformed by the grace of God. It is not, in Vos's terms, 'law-observance' in the meritorious sense, but it is certainly 'law-observance' (works, obedience, faithfulness) 'appropriate' to the life of a redeemed person. And if (1) one does not make the error of playing grace against human agency, and (2) one can avoid equating 'necessity' with the notion of autonomous works, obedience and faithfulness that merit God's favour, then it is possible to speak meaningfully of the necessity of works, obedience and faithfulness in the Christian life, without in any way compromising *sola fide* and the radical nature of divine grace.

Thus Vos continues to speak of the law 'not as the burden and yoke which it later came to be in the religious experience of the Jews, but as one of the greatest blessings and distinctions that Jehovah had conferred on his people'.[39] So, with Vos, we should not 'identify the Old Testament with law, negatively considered, and the New Testament with gospel'.[40] Indeed, Vos's perspective, at least at this point, is the perspective of this book. Thus there was indeed 'real gospel under

[38] Ibid. 127; emphasis original.
[39] Ibid. 128.
[40] Ibid.

the Theocracy'.[41] Vos is worth quoting at length when he writes about the presence of grace and even of 'gospel' in the Mosaic administration:

> The people of God of those days did not live and die under an unworkable, unredemptive system of religion, that could not give real access to and spiritual contact with God. Nor was this gospel-element contained exclusively in the revelation that preceded, accompanied, and followed the law; it is found *in the law itself.* That which we call 'the legal system' is shot through with strands of gospel and grace and faith. Especially the ritual law is rich in them. Every sacrifice and every lustration proclaimed the principle of grace. Had it been otherwise, then the idea of positive, vital continuity would have to be abandoned. There would be conflict and opposition instead. Such is the Gnostic position, but it is not the view either of the Old Testament itself, or of Paul, or of the Church theology.[42]

Vos affirms, as do I, that works and grace are not necessarily in conflict. I do not see how it is possible to make sense of the biblical material any other way. God is a God who saves by grace, expects his people to obey him, and moves his people to obey him. This obedience can be 'necessary' without compromising in the least an affirmation of the radical grace of God.

The law is not of faith – but is there grace within the law?

We now turn to portions of Scripture where the law is spoken of in extremely negative terms; indeed, where it is apparently spoken of as *against* faith, or *not of* faith. One of the most important passages in this regard is Galatians 3:12.

Galatians 3:10–12

The *locus classicus* for the relationship of promise (to Abraham), law (given to Moses) and the gospel, is Galatians 3:12, where Paul states

---

[41] Ibid.

[42] Ibid. 129; emphasis original. However, it is fascinating that Vos apparently retreats from this position, and emphasizes still the 'legal character' of the Mosaic administration. And because of this legal character of the Mosaic administration, it differs 'from the form it [God's revelation] exhibits at the present time' (ibid.).

that 'the law is not of faith'. In both Galatians 3:12 and Romans 10:5 Paul makes use of Leviticus 18:5. It is important to come to terms with what is being communicated in this nexus of passages. Let us start with Leviticus 18:5.

Placing Leviticus 18:5 in context, we note that 18:4 reads, 'You shall follow my rules and keep my statutes and walk in them. I am the LORD your God.' Then 18:5 reads, 'You shall therefore keep my statutes and my rules; if a person does them, he shall live by them: I am the LORD.' There is of course debate on how to make sense of the reference to Leviticus 18:5 in Galatians.[43] There are at least three key questions involved in making sense of the use of Leviticus 18:5: (1) What was the original purpose of Leviticus 18:5? (2) How was Paul using Leviticus 18:5 in Romans 10:5? And (3) how was Paul using Leviticus 18:5 in Galatians 3:12? In the Old Testament context itself, it seems unlikely that the Lord is setting forth a 'works covenant' or 'works' option by which one could merit salvation, justify oneself, and so on. More likely, the Lord is instructing his people that (1) he is the covenant God, (2) he expects his people to obey his word, and (3) there are blessings that follow upon obeying God.

When we move to the New Testament usage of this key passage, different issues arise. For example, how is Paul using this passage for his own purposes? Since my goal here is limited, I cannot offer anything near an exhaustive treatment. Certainly, whatever Paul means in Galatians 3:12, he cannot mean that faith was completely absent from the Old Testament era, including the Mosaic administration. In Hebrews 11 both Abraham and Moses are held up as exemplars of faith (cf. Heb. 11:8–31).[44] Paul cannot be comparing two legitimate paths to justification: that is, an Old Testament path via works, and a New Testament path via faith.[45] It is clear that Leviticus 18:5 is not laying out a recommended path of justification.[46] Rather, it speaks clearly about the life of faith when one is in covenant with God. To complicate Galatians 3:12 slightly, Paul quotes Habakkuk

---

[43] See Sprinkle: 2008.

[44] I know some might flinch at using Hebrews to help understand Paul. I am simply trying to operate within the *analogia fidei*, or the *analogia Scripturae*: Scripture must be interpreted by Scripture (see Blocher 1987).

[45] When I speak of 'legitimate' or 'suggested' paths to justification, I am proposing that God never intended humans to be justified by works.

[46] It is another question whether a works path to justification is implicit in Lev. 18:5. That is, it is conceivable (if unlikely) that Lev. 18:5 implies that if someone chose (however foolishly!) to seek justification by works, and was able to obey all of God's commands completely, that person could in fact be justified that way. No one is able to do such a thing; thus the only option is justification by faith.

2:4, which also speaks straightforwardly about the life of faith when one is in covenant with God. Thus, in their own contexts, both Leviticus 18:5 and Habakkuk 2:4 speak simply of the life of faith – a faith that works and obeys – when one is in covenant with God. That is, God graciously brings people into covenant relationship with him, and once they are in such a relationship, he gives commands and statutes – all of which must be obeyed.

But in Galatians 3:12 Paul is working in a different context with different purposes. We can see from Galatians 3:10 that he is concerned to refute those who 'rely on works of the law'. Such persons are under a curse because they believe one should approach God via works. But since Deuteronomy 27:26 teaches, 'Cursed be anyone who does not confirm the words of this law by doing them,' anyone who tries to approach God in such a works-centred way is indeed under a curse, for it is impossible to come to him that way. Indeed, as Paul continues in 3:11, '*no one* is justified before God by the law'. And then Paul turns to Habakkuk 2:4 and Leviticus 18:5, passages that both clearly speak of the life of faith.

Paul and the entire canon teach that in the new covenant God's people obey his will from the heart, because he has put his Spirit in them, has united them to Christ (by faith alone), and through his Spirit causes them to walk in his ways and keep his statutes.[47]

---

[47] To make sense of Paul's statement that 'the law is not of faith' almost requires one to sketch a biblical theology of the law more generally. My brief sketch would run something as follows (here I am relying on the insights of Blocher 2001: 121–123). Professor Blocher was kind enough to provide a translation and summary of this portion of his work. In one sense God's law is simply his moral expectations. His law is neither legalistic nor onerous, and its purpose is not primarily a foil to drive us to the gospel. God creates man, places him in the garden and communicates his will. This is fundamentally an act of God's goodness and righteousness. But after the entrance of sin into the world, law can function in different ways. As Blocher notes in his personal communication to me, after the entrance of sin into the world, the law 'denounces evil as evil'. But 'this new function is no new meaning; it is a logical corollary: as it defines righteousness, it defines (and so denounces) unrighteousness'. Considered in our relationship to God, then, 'law' is simply God's will lovingly revealed to us both for his glory and our good. When does the issue of 'legalism' enter the scene? As Blocher sees it, 'Legalism begins when sinners, who are found under the regime of law, imagine they can, *by doing works prescribed by the law, obtain life, acceptance with God*' (emphasis original). To the extent that one seeks acceptance before God by one's law-keeping, one certainly is under the curse of the law: for no one (except Jesus, the obedient Son) obeys the Father perfectly. But this is not because the law is designed to frustrate persons or be a curse. The law itself is holy, righteous and good (Rom. 7:7, 12). It even (when properly approached!) revives the soul (Ps. 19:7). Once someone is in covenant relationship with God, his will (a part of which is expressed in his law) ought to be obeyed – *mutatis mutandis* in terms of the historical-redemptive shift as one moves from old to new covenant, from the era of promise and shadows to the era of fulfilment and

Faith itself is simply part and parcel of the life of the believer in both Old and New Testament. Paul does not say in Galatians 3:12 that faith has emerged in the first century. Rather, it would seem that he is saying that 'law' – shorthand for the attempt to find acceptance with God by law-keeping – is not of faith. There are two main 'whole-Bible' theology reasons in favour of my position. First, across the entire canon God saves first by grace and then gives commands. There is no place in Scripture where the primary way of acceptance with God is law-keeping. Secondly, this understanding fits Paul's teaching in passages such as Romans 9:30–33. In Romans 9:30–33, Paul deals with a tough question: Why did the Jews (generally) not reach 'a law that would lead to righteousness' (9:31)? Paul certainly does not argue that Israel failed because of some fundamental problem with the law (may it never be! Cf. Rom. 7:7, 10, 12). Rather, Israel failed because they did not pursue a law that would lead to righteousness *by faith*. Instead, they pursued the law that would lead to righteousness 'as if it were based on works' (9:32).

So the problem in Galatians 3:12 is not fundamentally or essentially the law itself. The problem is with the people and with their approach to the law. The law in every era of redemptive history was to be approached by faith. True righteousness is by faith. The law is 'not of faith' because faith always should come first, and our obedience to the law should always be a faith-filled, Spirit-induced obedience to the commands of God. The law was never meant to be a way of justification or acceptance before God. When someone approaches the law apart from or without faith, or approaches the law believing that one can obey all of God's commands in any sort of autonomous capacity, this person has completely misunderstood the whole structure of grace and obedience. God's commands are good and gracious and have

reality (Heb. 8:5; 10:1). God's law, transposed into a new covenant key, should indeed be obeyed. One cannot forget that in the one place in the OT where the term 'new covenant' is used (Jer. 31:31–34), a central mark of the new covenant is that God will place his law within his covenant people and will write it on their hearts (Jer. 31:33). Through the Holy Spirit, and through the power of the cross and resurrection itself, mediated to us because of the perpetual priesthood of the risen Jesus, God's people have the spiritual ability to obey him. Jesus has obeyed the Father in our place (he is indeed the obedient Son, the obedient Messiah), but his obedience for us does not negate the centrality of the obedience of God's covenant people. On the contrary, Jesus' obedience for us is the ground and foundation of our obedience. Our obedience to the Father flows from Jesus' obedience to the Father. As Blocher writes, 'Under the new regime, they [the people of God] live and are accepted by the works/obedience of Another, who substituted for them, even under punishment. *Under the regime of faith, grace, gospel, they obey the norms of God*, as the ways of life, but they are no longer under the regime of law' (emphasis original).

always been meant to be approached by the person of faith. If one chooses to approach the law apart from faith, or one believes one can obey all of God's law in an autonomous way, then one has completely missed the place of the law and has misunderstood the priority and centrality of faith in approaching God.

Excursus: John Owen on the covenant

I include here some key insights from John Owen on the nature of the covenant, and particularly the nature of the *new* covenant. Surely John Owen is right when he writes, 'all theology . . . is founded on covenant'.[48] Our interest in Owen lies in the significant attention and commentary he gives to Hebrews 8:6: 'But as it is, Christ has obtained a ministry that is as much more excellent than the old as the covenant he mediates is better, since it is enacted on better promises.'

One of the key issues is the 'newness' of the new covenant. Owen is a helpful dialogue partner at this point because he is clearly working within the Reformed tradition, but also offers a 'minority report' of sorts within that tradition, while attempting to wrestle with the 'newness' of the new covenant. Owen rightly links the superiority of the new covenant with the superiority of its priest, Christ. This is of course exactly what the writer to the Hebrews is arguing: a better priest means a better covenant (Heb. 7 – 10). But this in itself does not necessarily mean that the new covenant is qualitatively better, although I argue that we get to this conclusion eventually (i.e. the new covenant is indeed a qualitatively better covenant).

When Owen speaks of the old covenant in Hebrews 8, he is speaking of the Mosaic covenant. And of particular interest is Owen's understanding of the role of grace in the Mosaic covenant (as well as the Adamic administration or covenant). Owen writes, 'There is infinite grace in every divine covenant.' Indeed, 'Infinite condescension it is in God, that he will enter covenant with dust and ashes, with poor worms of the earth. And herein lies the spring of all grace, from whence all the streams of it do flow.'[49] Gatiss summarizes Owen, 'the same reward (and penalty) was offered by the covenant of works as by the new covenant, and Adam's immortality was secured only by the most free goodwill of God'.[50] On the graciousness of the Adamic administration/covenant, Gatiss notes:

---

[48] Owen 1661: 44; quoted in Gatiss 2013: 154.
[49] Owen 1991: 6:68; quoted in Gatiss 2013: 170.
[50] Ibid. 171.

For Owen, there is a measure of undeserved, unmerited (and unmeritable) grace within the graciously bestowed covenant with Adam. There is also disproportionality between obedience and proposed rewards which 'were, indeed, also of grace, in that the reward did infinitely exceed the merit of our obedience.'[51]

As Owen continues, 'the promise . . . of eternal life with God, did in strict justice exceed the worth of the obedience required, and so was a superadded effect of goodness and grace'.[52] Finally, Owen writes that the covenant of works 'had in it exceeding mixture of goodness and grace, both in the obedience constituted in it and the reward annexed unto it'.[53]

As Lee Gatiss has noted, perhaps the most crucial component of Owen's understanding of the 'newness' or 'improvement' of the new covenant lies in a certain historical-redemptive shift that takes place in the first century. This shift relates to the usage of *nenomothetētai* (be enacted) in Hebrews 8:6. Owen's key insight is that the new covenant existed in the form of promise during the Old Testament era, but was completed and established in the first century with the death, burial and resurrection of Jesus. As Owen writes:

> That which before lay hid in promises, in many things obscure, the principal mysteries of it being a secret hid in God himself, was now brought to light; and that covenant which had invisibly, in the way of a promise, put forth its efficacy under types and shadows, was now solemnly sealed, ratified, and confirmed, in the death and resurrection of Christ. It had before the confirmation of a promise, which is an oath; it had now the confirmation of a covenant, which is blood. That which before had no visible, outward worship, proper and peculiar unto it, is now made the only rule and instrument of worship unto the whole church, nothing being to be admitted therein but what belongs unto it, and is appointed by it. This the apostle intends by *nenomothetētai*, the 'legal establishment' of the new covenant, with all the ordinances of its worship.[54]

Interestingly, when one says that the covenant of grace is (1) at one point promised (in the OT era), and (2) at another point legally

---

51 Owen 1991, 6: 69 (cf. 6: 66); quoted in Gatiss 2013: 172.
52 Owen 1991, 2: 345; quoted in Gatiss 2013: 172.
53 Owen 1965, 14: 184; quoted in Gatiss 2013: 174.
54 Owen 1991, 6: 64; quoted in Gatiss 2013: 177.

established (in the NT era – with the death, burial and resurrection of Jesus), the pressure to posit an atemporal 'covenant of grace' which is then manifested in different historical covenants (Abraham, Moses, David, New) is diminished. That is, there is quite a difference in saying there is an atemporal 'covenant of grace' which is manifested in different historical covenants (Abraham, Moses, David, new) than saying there is a historical 'covenant of grace' promised in the Old Testament era and established in the New Testament era.

Of especial interest to the argument of this monograph is how Owen understands conditions and obedience in the covenant of grace. As Gatiss summarizes:

> The covenant of grace is not without conditions in the sense that God requires obedience in it yet 'the principal promises thereof' are not in the first place *remunerative* of our obedience in the covenant, but *efficaciously assumptive* of us into the covenant, and establishing or confirming in the covenant.[55]

As Gatiss concludes, 'the covenant of grace gives us the things promised before we have obeyed, even the faith by which we receive forgiveness (which is not to be considered, therefore, a reward for faith)'.[56]

The chief insights of Owen for our purposes are as follows.

First, he appropriately sees grace in the Old Testament era and affirms that this grace is linked to the death, burial and resurrection of Jesus. Hence Owen speaks of the promise of the new covenant existing in the Old Testament era and the established new covenant in the New Testament era. Thus one can be saved by grace in the Old Testament era; but this grace is Christ-centred and gospel-centred, in that the Old Testament saints are being saved, ultimately, by the death of Christ promised or foreshadowed even though they live in the Old Testament era, under the old covenant.

Secondly, contra other Reformed thinkers who would see the Mosaic covenant as fundamentally a covenant of grace (or a manifestation of the covenant of grace), Owen sees the Mosaic covenant (or old covenant) as 'declaring' the covenant of works. Owen is not using 'republication' language (where the Mosaic covenant is a 'republication' – a reprinting – of the covenant of works), but, because

---

[55] Owen 1991, 6: 69; quoted in Gatiss 2013: 181; emphasis original.
[56] Gatiss 2013: 181.

he is trying to be faithful to the 'better covenant' language of New Testament passages like Heb. 8 – 9, he distinguishes between the old covenant and the new.

Thirdly, for Owen, the covenant of grace 'flowers' into the new covenant, while the old (Mosaic) covenant is a different covenant. The covenant of works as a covenant is technically a covenant that ended with Adam's failure to keep it.

Owen is a giant in the world of theology, and I differ from him with some trepidation. However, part of the work of biblical theology, particularly if one is committed to the Reformation principle of *semper reformanda* (always to be reformed), is to challenge, when necessary, certain received theological formulations. With Owen we can affirm that the 'better covenant' language of the New Testament (esp. Heb. 8 – 9) inclines us to make sense of what exactly is 'better' and 'new' about the new covenant. And since Owen desires to root the forgiveness of sins and the salvation of sinners in the person and work of Christ, it seems biblical and therefore wise to draw out the links between forgiveness during the Old Testament era and the death, burial and resurrection of Jesus. Hence Owen's idea that there was a promise of the new covenant in the Old Testament era that is established in the New Testament era seems to move in the right direction.

However, it seems unnecessary to posit a covenant of works that is then 'declared' again (but not necessarily 'republished') in the Mosaic covenant. Indeed, it may be the case that Owen's Reformed peers – who tended to see the Mosaic covenant as a covenant of grace – were on to something. Some of the tension here is the tendency to link works with a works-covenant of some sorts. If it is the case that 'works' are what flow from the heart of the person who trusts in the God of holy Scripture, it quickly becomes unnecessary to make recourse to a 'covenant of works' when we see mention of works (e.g. in the Mosaic covenant). However, if in every covenantal relationship with the Lord – from Adam to the new covenant – the sovereign, covenant Lord calls his people to obey him, then the theological pressure to link 'works' with a 'covenant of works' lessens. When God calls a people to himself, he calls them to obey him. And he saves first by grace and then calls his people to obey, or in the case of his relationship with Adam, creates Adam and supplies all his need; Adam did not at that point need to be saved. Thus we need not be skittish when we see God's commands.

This by no means settles the issue, and we cannot skirt difficult questions. There does appear to be a newness to the new covenant that exists at the level of quality and not just quantity. But to affirm that the new covenant is qualitatively better than the old does not necessarily require a strong law–gospel contrast. We can argue that (1) God always saves by grace, (2) he requires obedience of all those who relate to him (whether in the OT or NT eras), (3) the death, burial and resurrection of Jesus is the fount of all forgiveness (and the fount of all mortification, sanctification, faithfulness, works and obedience), (4) the new covenant is quantitatively better than the old (all covenant members have circumcised hearts and are regenerate), and (5) the new covenant is qualitatively superior with a better priest, better promises, a better sacrifice and a more substantial pouring out of the Holy Spirit.

Conclusion

One of the goals of biblical theology is to understand the Bible's big picture in the light of its particulars, and the particulars in the light of the big picture – in short, to understand the overarching story line and meaning of the Bible without running roughshod over its specific teachings and stories. One of the key issues in this regard is the nature of biblical covenants, and in particular the continuity and discontinuity between the old and new covenant. In this chapter I have attempted to flesh out some of the key issues concerning the newness of the new covenant and the complementary relationship of law and gospel. There is development as one moves from old to new covenant: the new is both quantitatively and qualitatively better than the old.

I have suggested that salvation is by grace across the entire canon, and that likewise there is the expectation of works, obedience and faithfulness across the entire canon. I have argued, in agreement with Henri Blocher, that while there is a fundamental continuity between old covenant and new, there is an 'advance' of sorts as one moves from old to new. I have also argued that one should not overreach in contrasting law and gospel, and, leaning on John Frame and Richard Gaffin, I have suggested that there is a grace within the law, and that the gospel does not free one from the obligation to obey our covenant Lord. The excursus on John Owen briefly explored some of his brilliant insights on the nature of the new covenant.

At the heart of biblical teaching is atonement. And in the New Testament the death of Christ for us is at the heart of the matter. Any understanding of works, obedience and faithfulness in the new covenant must link them to the atoning work of Christ, to which we now turn.

Chapter Four

The cross and the reality of works, obedience and faithfulness

For a number of years I have taught university undergraduates. These are bright young people, and a good number of them come to college with a seemingly genuine and heartfelt piety, and with a desire to serve the Lord. They are excited to learn, and many desire to delve deeper into the Scriptures. They understand, to some degree, that they have been saved by grace. However, if you dig deeper, and seek to discern their thinking on the Christian life, on the quest for holiness, one runs into rockier ground. In particular, there is often little ability to link one's ongoing relationship with Christ – including the quest for holiness – to the gospel. This weakness, at least in my experience, seems to be manifest in many churches. I want to suggest that it is crucial to link one's ongoing relationship with the Lord, one's ongoing quest for holiness, to the gospel. Specifically, I want to suggest that our continued obedience and growth in Christ is something that flows from the cross. I also want to emphasize that I do not see myself being original here in the least. Like Tom Oden, I desire to be particularly unoriginal in 'doing theology' – at least most of the time.[1]

In this chapter we will look at key texts where there are links between the atoning work of Christ and our works, obedience and faithfulness. Some of these links are explicit, but others less so.

Key biblical texts

Romans 8:3–4

Romans 8:3–4 is a striking passage, both for what it says, and for what it does not say:

[1] Oden 1990.

For God has done what the law, weakened by the flesh, could not do. By sending his own Son in the likeness of sinful flesh and for sin, he condemned sin in the flesh, in order that the righteous requirement of the law might be fulfilled in us, who walk not according to the flesh but according to the Spirit.

In his critique of N. T. Wright, John Piper devotes an appendix to Romans 8:4, and understandably so.[2] Piper correctly notes that Paul is not (simply) saying that Jesus kept the law for us. From other biblical passages, we do know that Christ kept the law for us. We could argue that because Christ kept the law for us, it is possible that the righteousness of the law might be fulfilled in us.[3] But we must be faithful to what Paul is saying here, in Romans 8:4.[4]

Even if we read Paul as teaching that somehow Christians – by the power of the Spirit, and flowing from the incarnation and atonement – are to 'fulfil' the law, 'fulfil' must nonetheless be interpreted in its historical-redemptive context. As Dunn rightly argues, 'It must mean "fulfill" in a more profound sense – the essential requirement (note again the singular) which lies behind the individual requirements, the character and purpose which the individual requirements are intended to bring to expression.'[5] Dunn concludes, 'Paul has in mind the role of the law as the standard or yardstick of what God wants, and so

---

[2] Piper 2007: 215–225.

[3] Cf. Dumbrell: 'The point for Paul is not the release from divine obligation, but that in this New Covenant era it should be given the proper inward direction (cf. 7:9–13) it always required' (2005: 86).

[4] Piper 2007: 225. Piper offers a threefold summary of his position, all of which resonates with the overall argument of this book: (1) '[O]ur imperfect love is, nevertheless, real, God-dependent, Spirit-enabled, Christ-exalting love that *flows from* our justification and is not a *means* to it. And therefore it is the new direction that the law was aiming at and what the new covenant promised. In short, *Christ-exalting love as the fruit of faith* is what the law was aiming at.'

(2) '[O]ur imperfect love is the firstfruits of a final perfection that Christ will complete in us at his appearing. Romans 8:4 does not say that the entire fulfillment of the law happens in us *now*. But our walk by the Spirit *begins* now, and so does our fulfillment of the righteous requirement of the law.'

(3) '[O]ur imperfect love is the fruit of our faith in Jesus who is himself our only justifying perfection before God. In other words, the only law-keeping we depend on as the ground of our justification is Jesus' law-keeping. His was perfect. Ours is imperfect. . . . In the end, the law is fulfilled in us everlastingly because it was fulfilled in him from everlasting to everlasting. Our imperfection and need is a pointer to his perfection and all-sufficiency; and that pointing – that exaltation of Christ – is the aim of the law' (emphases original).

[5] Dunn 1988: 423.

of a "doing" or "keeping" ("fulfilling," 13:8–10) of the law in some positive sense.'[6]

Peter Stuhlmacher argues as well, 'Through the sacrifice of Christ, those who believe fulfill the legal demand of the law, which takes place in the power of the Spirit.'[7] Stuhlmacher likewise looks to Ezekiel 36 and Jeremiah 31:

> for the sake of the sacrificial death of Jesus, God no longer considers sinners to belong to those who have deviated from the law (cf. Jer. 31:32, 34). Rather, they now participate in the obedience of Christ in the power of the Holy Spirit, who indwells them since their baptism, and in the power of Christ (cf. Jer. 31:31–34; Ezek. 36:27) fulfill the will of God which has been given to them anew in their hearts by the resurrected Lord.[8]

Stuhlmacher continues, Paul 'teaches how the breakthrough of the new revelation and spiritual internalization of the instruction of God promised in Jeremiah 31:31–34 comes about in and through Christ and how this instruction is then followed by Christians in the power of the Spirit!'[9]

Charles Hodge is not convinced that the actions of the human person are in view. He argues that Romans 8:4 must ultimately be speaking about declarative justification. 'This verse must refer to justification and not sanctification. He condemned sin in order that the demands of the law might be satisfied.'[10]

John Calvin likewise seems troubled by the notion that Paul is teaching that we fulfil the law in any meaningful way. Calvin writes, 'They who understand that the renewed, by the Spirit of Christ, fulfil the law, introduce a gloss wholly alien to the meaning of Paul; for the

---

[6] Ibid. 424.
[7] Stuhlmacher 1994: 120.
[8] Ibid.
[9] Ibid. 121.
[10] Hodge 1993: 232. Hodge (232–233) lists several reasons for this. First, this is 'consistent with the strict and natural meaning of the words' ('righteousness' in context would seem to require a declarative sense). Secondly, the analogy of Scripture discourages seeing this passage as teaching an actual 'fulfilment' of the law by Christians (what Hodge calls 'subjective justification'). Thirdly, since the last clause of this passage speaks of those 'who do not live according to the sinful nature', it is better to read the passage as denoting justification, or else Paul is being redundant: 'Christ died in order that they should be holy who are holy.' Fourthly, believers in fact do not fulfil the 'righteous requirement of the Law'; thus, Paul must be speaking of something else (forensic justification).

faithful, while they sojourn in this world, never make such a proficiency, as that the justification of the law becomes in them full or complete.'[11]

Henri Blocher is understandably struck by the massive implications of Romans 8:4. He writes, 'What a paradox! The law, which focuses on holy obedience is unable to secure that obedience, it is powerless as regards sanctification just as it is for justification – but faith that justifies without works makes sanctification possible and actual!'[12]

With some interpreters (Blocher, Piper, Stuhlmacher) and, to some degree, against such titans as John Calvin and Charles Hodge, I simply note that flowing from the cross is *some kind of real ability* to 'fulfil the righteous requirement of the law'. Although this monograph is not another attempt to wrestle with all the thorny issues related to Paul and the law, it is impossible to ignore such issues. For the present, I affirm that in the new covenant the atoning work of Christ does not merely allow us to cross a line from death to life (John 5:24). It is certainly no less than that. But flowing from the cross of Christ is a real ability to obey the Lord. This ability can even be described in terms of 'fulfilling' the righteous requirement of the law. God sent his Son as an offering, and therefore sin was condemned, with the result that the requirement of God's law 'might be fulfilled in us'. While we might expect Paul to say something like, 'so that the requirement of the law might be fulfilled *for* us'; rather, he says '*in* us' (*en hēmin*).[13] The key insight in Romans 8:3–4, for our purposes, is that the atoning work of Christ results in a real internal change in the people of God. Indeed, the righteous requirements of the law are met in the believer.[14]

Romans 8:13–14

Romans 8:13–14 is another key passage. John Owen, in his book on mortification, appropriates Romans 8:13–14 as a theme verse, and spends much of his treatise wrestling with this passage. In 8:13–14

[11] Calvin 1981, 19: 283.

[12] Blocher 2011: 12.

[13] It is of course necessary to be careful how much 'weight' one places on prepositions, as argued in the classic essay by Harris (1978). Now see Harris 2012.

[14] Rosner (2013: 121–123) affirms the forensic element present in Rom. 8:3–4 (as I do), but is more cautious about this passage having much to do with what we do. Hence he writes, 'The just demand of the law is fulfilled, or brought to completion *in us*, not by us' (123; emphasis original). Following Moo 1996: 483, he writes, 'The passive voice of *plēroō* in Romans 8:4 ("so that the just requirement of the law *might be fulfilled* in us") "points not to something we are to do but to something that is done in and for us".' And Rosner sees the issue of the reality of the human agent, for in the very next paragraph he affirms, 'the fulfillment of the law is not accomplished only *for believers, but also through believers*' (123).

Paul writes, 'For if you live according to the flesh, you will die, but if by the Spirit you put to death the deeds of the body, you will live. For all who are led by the Spirit of God are sons of God.' Owen makes the case that mortification, or the putting to death of the old man, is necessary. That is, it is something that must happen. If the believer wishes to live, there must be a real putting to death of the old man. Owen argues that this mortification takes place by the power of the Spirit. We should pay attention whenever we see 'conditions' like these in the New Testament. The condition of putting to death the deeds of the body by the Spirit appears to be something *we* must do, if we expect to live. And indeed, Owen argues along these very lines. If his understanding is correct, then a very basic question emerges: Can we say that we are 'saved by grace alone', that we are 'saved by faith alone'? Owen writes:

> Mortification of sin is peculiarly from the death of Christ. It is one peculiar, yea, eminent end of the death of Christ, which shall assuredly be accomplished by it. He died to destroy the works of the devil; whatever came upon our natures by his first temptation, whatever received strength in our persons by his daily suggestions, Christ died to destroy it all.[15]

Or likewise, can we really say there are no 'conditions' besides faith for our salvation? That is, are we forced to say – with Francis Turretin and many others – that works are necessary for salvation?

Owen argues, as this book does, that our putting to death the deeds of the body, by the Spirit, is a reality that flows from the cross. Towards the end of the treatise Owen references Hebrews 2:18: 'For since He Himself was tempted in that which He has suffered, He is able to come to the aid of those who are tempted' (NASB). In short, Jesus' 'ability' to help us flows from his sufferings on the cross. Owen writes, 'And this, by virtue of his death, in various and several degrees, shall be accomplished. Hence, our washing, purging and cleansing, is everywhere ascribed to his blood (1 John 1:7; Heb. 1:3; Rev. 1:5).'[16] He continues, 'Christ, by his death, destroying the works of the devil, procuring the Spirit for us, hath so killed sin as to its reign in believers, that it shall not obtain its end and dominion.'[17] Owen references Titus 2:14, where it is Christ 'who gave himself for us to redeem us from all

[15] Owen 1965, 6: 83.
[16] Ibid.
[17] Ibid. 85.

lawlessness and to purify for himself a people for his own possession who are zealous for good works'. Likewise, in Ephesians 5:26–27 Christ dies for the church 'that he might sanctify her, having cleansed her by the washing of water with the word, so that he might present the church to himself in splendour, without spot or wrinkle or any such thing, that she might be holy and without blemish'.

In his own gloss on Romans 6:2 ('How can we who died to sin still live in it?'), Owen writes, 'Dead to sin by profession; dead to sin by obligation to be so; dead to sin by participation of virtue and power for the killing of it; dead to sin by union and interest in Christ, in and by whom it is killed: how shall we live therein?'[18] Owen continues, 'The Spirit alone brings the *cross* of Christ into our hearts with its sin-killing power; for by the Spirit are we baptized into the death of Christ.'[19]

Owen's fundamental insights are undeniable. Mortification is necessary in the Christian life. Mortification is also something that flows from the death of Christ, and is brought about by the Holy Spirit. And note that the agency, or working, of the Holy Spirit does not negate the reality or need for human agency. Rather, it is better to say that the agency of the Holy Spirit is that which efficaciously brings about human agency in mortification.

2 Corinthians 4:7–12

This passage is an important one for my argument. Paul asserts that 'we' (Paul and his co-workers) are always 'carrying in the body the death of Jesus, so that the life of Jesus may also be manifested in our bodies' (v. 10). Interestingly, Paul then goes on to argue that 'we' are 'always being given over to death for Jesus' sake, so that the life of Jesus also may be manifested in our mortal flesh' (v. 12). There are at least a couple of important issues to note here. First, for Paul it is the death of Jesus (which we 'carry') that leads to the manifestation (in our bodies) of the life of Jesus (v. 10). Secondly, Paul restates this (from a slightly different angle) in verse 11, where he says that we are being given over to death – for Jesus' sake – so that there might be a manifestation of the life of Jesus in 'our' mortal flesh.

For Paul, it is through (and because of) the death of Jesus that Jesus' life is manifested in us. The death of Jesus is first and foremost *extra nos* – 'outside us'. The external reality of his death, if appropriated by

[18] Ibid. 84.
[19] Ibid. 86; emphasis original.

faith alone, unavoidably leads to the life of Jesus being manifested in us. Paul's teaching is markedly similar to that of Jesus: that we save our life only if we give it up (cf. Matt. 10:39; 16:25; Mark 8:35; Luke 9:24; 17:33; John 12:25). We experience life because of the death of Jesus. The Christian (if we apply Paul's experience, here at least, to the common Christian, the necessary changes being made)[20] is being given over to death (for Jesus' sake) so that the life of Jesus might be a reality in the life of the believer.

It should be noted that while I am engaging with this passage in the chapter on the atonement, it could also have been addressed in the chapter on union with Christ. Paul is arguing that the Christian's life is radically shaped and informed by the cross. Indeed, it is fashionable today to speak of the 'cruciform' life – but it is not untrue for being fashionable. Undergirding Paul's theology is the belief that those in union with Christ find the life, death and resurrection of Christ mysteriously replicated in their own lives. The Christian is 'in Christ', and Christ is 'in' the Christian. Where the head goes the body will follow. And in this life the Christian suffers – not by accident, nor in a meritorious sense, and not simply due to sin in general. The Christian is promised suffering (2 Tim. 3:12). And somehow the suffering of Christians is analogous to the suffering of their Lord. As Barnett concludes:

> the very 'dying' and 'life' of Jesus continue and are extended in time in the missionary sufferings, and deliverances from those sufferings, in the experience of the apostles. It is by this twin reality of suffering and deliverance in the lives of the slaves of the Slave (v. 5), and only by means of it, that the true character of Christ's unique salvation was and continues to be manifested in the world and extended into history until the appearing of Christ.[21]

Ephesians 5:25–27

In Ephesians 5:25 Paul instructs husbands to 'love your wives, as Christ loved the church and gave himself up for her'. But Paul does not simply issue this teaching as an abstract reality. A husband is to love his wife as Christ loved the church, and gave himself up for her '*that* he might sanctify her, having cleansed her by the washing of water with the word, *so that* he might present the church to himself

---

[20] On the applicability of the realities in this passage to the common Christian, see Barnett 1997: 229–232.
[21] Ibid. 236.

in splendour, without spot or wrinkle or any such thing, that she might be holy and without blemish' (vv. 26–27). In short, Paul contends:

- Husbands are to love their wives as Christ loved the church.
- Christ loved the church so much that he gave up his life for her.
- Christ gave up his life for the church in order to accomplish certain things.
- In particular: Christ died for the church because in so doing he was providing that which would – ultimately – be the fount of his bride's (the church's) holiness and cleansing, because . . .
- this bride will one day be presented to the bridegroom as a holy bride without blemish.

So, if in reading Paul we simply stop with the fact that Christ loved the church enough to die for her, we will have truncated Paul's message – even though that abbreviated message alone is already good news! But Paul's point is a larger one. The long-term goal is the sanctification of a bride to be presented to the bridegroom – and the preparation of the bride is fundamentally something that flows from the cross of Christ.[22] So we see in this text that the cross of Christ is not simply something that provides the grounds for entering into covenant relationship with God (it is certainly not less than that). Although the cross is the fount of our cleansing and holiness, our own works, obedience and faithfulness play a part in our sanctification. One of the most common ways the Old Testament portrays Israel's disobedience is in terms of marital infidelity (see esp. Jer. 2:1 – 6:30).

Hebrews 10:10, 14

Hebrews 10 is a crucial passage for grasping the relationship between the cross and the Christian life. Peter O'Brien has written, 'Christ's intercessions cover anything and everything that will enable God's children to persevere and receive the final salvation Christ has won

---

[22] Erasmus Sarcerius (1542: no p.) wrote in his *Annotations on Ephesians*, 'The sanctification of the church is the work of the surrender, suffering and death of Christ, and not of the works and merits of the church itself. The church would not need Christ's work of sanctification if it could sanctify itself by its own works and merits.' Calvin, in his commentary on Ephesians writes, 'Note that the church is to be holy, not for the sake of other people but for the sake of Christ.' He continues, 'Paul does not mean that the church has achieved perfection already but merely states the purpose for which Christ has cleansed it.' Indeed, 'The church has started along the road to holiness and makes further progress every day' (quoted in Bray 2011: 386).

for them at the cross (see on 7:25).'[23] This insight is vindicated as we look across the New Testament. Hebrews 10:10 reads, 'And by that will we have been sanctified through the offering of the body of Jesus Christ once for all.' That is, we were sanctified (perfect passive participle of *hagiazō*), or set apart, by the cross. Similarly, in Hebrews 10:14, 'For by a single offering he has perfected [*teteleiōken*] for all time those who are being sanctified [*hagiazomenous*].' The logic of Hebrews 10:10 and 14 appears to be that (1) we are set apart ('positionally' or 'definitively' sanctified) by the cross, which leads to (2) our ongoing ('progressive') sanctification, which also flows from the cross. Both (1) our initial act of being set apart and (2) our ongoing growth in holiness are realities rooted in the cross. As Vos writes of Hebrews 10:10, 'the Messiah received a body that He might be able to offer it up in death and thus fulfill the will of God relative to his death. And in this will of God, carried out by Jesus, lies the cause of our sanctification.'[24]

Now, if our holiness is rooted in the cross, we have a glorious and life-giving insight that can help the church as it calls for holiness and encourages the flock to faithfulness. If we work with a paradigm that sees grace as simply 'getting us in', we will be unable to make the connection between the cross and the rest of the Christian life. Thus we end up with – in John Piper's words – a 'debtor's ethic': namely, we have been saved by grace, and now we spend the rest of our lives paying God back.[25] Instead, a cross-centred understanding of our obedience contends that the power of the cross not merely 'gets us in', but is also the means of our continued obedience. And the consequences of severing our quest for holiness from the cross are weighty indeed. If we see our quest for holiness as being up to our own efforts, we will probably either give up or become legalists (and legalists, it seems to me, are often simply folks who have given up on the quest for holiness but do not admit this to others).

Tom Schreiner argues similarly, 'The obedience of believers has its basis in the work of Christ on the cross, and this provides the platform on which believers receive ability to keep the law.'[26] Schreiner continues, 'The Pauline theme of obedience should not be identified as a new legalism, for the new obedience is the work of the Spirit in those who are the new creation work of Christ. The work of the cross is not

---

[23] O'Brien 2010: 339.
[24] Vos 1980b: 216.
[25] See Piper 1995: ch. 1.
[26] Schreiner 1998: 405. Schreiner here references the work of Reinmuth (1985: 70).

diminished, for *the cross is the basis and foundation for the transforming work of the Spirit in us.*'[27]

Christ's righteousness and our righteousness

The most contentious issue in all of this will be how to construe the relationship between Christ's righteousness and 'righteousness' or works, obedience or faithfulness found in believers. Again, it is a dodge to treat all commands to obey as simply commands that point to our own inability, and therefore point us to Christ's righteousness. That is, I suspect we cannot treat every command to obey in the sense of the 'second use' of the law: its elenctic (refuting) or pedagogic use – where the demands of the law simply 'refute' or lead us from law to gospel. Rather, the New Testament writers link loving Jesus with obeying him, and Christians do love Jesus, if imperfectly, short of the eschaton. God expects those who confess the lordship of Christ to be marked by real, if imperfect, works, obedience and faithfulness.

That being said, in a relationship begun and governed by God's sovereign grace, God expects his people to obey him. In the new covenant God gives commands to his people, but they know they can never obey him by their own autonomous wills. Rather, by being united with Christ by faith alone, and since Christ is being formed in them (Gal. 4:19), believers' obedience is something graciously elicited by a good and sovereign God, and this obedience is organically and mysteriously a result of – or linked to – Christ dwelling in the believer. Thus the commands of God 'refute' and 'tutor' us as they point us to Christ, the ultimate law-keeper. However, since Christ, the capital 'L' Law-keeper, is now being formed in us, and dwells – through the Spirit – in us, we are now lower-case 'l' law-keepers.

Here I am not entering the debate about whether justification should be construed as 'transformative' in addition to being 'forensic'. For example, Peter Leithart has argued that at times justification language is not only forensic, but denotes deliverance as well.[28] My argument does not require a recasting of the traditional Protestant understanding of justification.[29] One may decide on exegetical grounds that justification should be construed as a 'transformative'

---

[27] Schreiner 2007: 95; emphasis original.
[28] Leithart 2007: 56–72; cf. Allen and Treier 2008: 105–110.
[29] On this issue see the excellent article by Blocher (2004).

reality as well as a 'forensic' reality, but that is not what I am doing here.

A traditional understanding of justification is fully compatible with my thesis – that in the new covenant the believer should be marked by a pattern of works, obedience and faithfulness. Indeed, as Blocher properly notes, the traditional Protestant understanding of justification is the necessary precondition of a biblical understanding of gospel-centred human transformation. It should be affirmed – as argued below – that the cross of Christ does in fact lead to a transformed life. Blocher is persuasive:

> Defenders of the traditional Protestant view will add of course, that the actual renewal, the new creation, is also given, and at the same time. Justification and regeneration go together (the logical order between the two, will be suggested below, can be read both ways). But as Calvin argues their coincidence does not entail that we may confuse the one with the other: no more than light and heat in sunshine.[30]

A brief look at Luther and Calvin

Luther, in his 'Two Kinds of Righteousness', clearly rooted our growth in holiness (the 'second' kind of righteousness) in the righteousness reckoned to us by faith (the 'first' kind of righteousness). That is, any growth or transformation that we experience flows from Christ's righteousness, which is reckoned to us by faith. I suggest – and this is not new – that it is essential to understand how the believer's works, obedience and faithfulness relate to Christ the obedient one. I have already suggested that one of the keys to a biblical understanding of union with Christ is that we must affirm that this union is by faith apart from works. Thus Paul writes in Ephesians 2:6 that God has 'raised us up with him and seated us with him in the heavenly places in Christ Jesus' (*synēgeiren kai synekathisen en tois epouraniois en Christō Iēsou*).

Calvin speaks of our works being 'reckoned' righteous. That is, he recognizes that the Scriptures speak of good works, and that the Father's continued blessings are somehow linked to our obedience. Calvin writes, 'Those whom the Lord has destined by his mercy for

---

[30] Ibid. 494. He continues, 'Only if an *alien* righteousness is credited to it, in other words, if justification is forensic, can our imperfect works, the mixture of righteousness and unrighteousness we can show, be graciously accepted by God' (495; emphasis original).

the inheritance of eternal life he leads into possession of it, according to his ordinary dispensation, by means of good works.'[31] Likewise:

> while through the intercession of Christ's righteousness God reconciles us to himself, and by free remission of sins accounts us righteous, his beneficence is at the same time joined with such a mercy that through his Holy Spirit he dwells in us and by his power the lusts of our flesh are each day more and more mortified; we are indeed sanctified, that is consecrated to the Lord in true purity of life, with our hearts formed to obedience to the law.[32]

Thus Calvin affirms the reality of 'works', but says that even these are – through saving faith – 'clothed in Christ'. Calvin writes:

> If these things are true, surely no works of ours can of themselves render us acceptable and pleasing to God; nor can even the works themselves please him, except to the extent that a man, covered by the righteousness of Christ, pleases God and obtains forgiveness of his sins.[33]

Imputation of Christ's righteousness

A great deal of contention swirls around the question of the imputation (or lack thereof) of Christ's active obedience.[34] One argument says that, since through faith we are united with Christ and thus his righteousness becomes ours through union with him, it is not necessary

[31] Calvin 1960: 3.14.21. Calvin is indeed concerned about persons who would see works as justifying anyone. He writes, 'This is the pivotal point of our disputation. For on the beginning of justification there is no quarrel between us and the sounder Schoolmen: that a sinner freely liberated from condemnation may obtain righteousness, and that through the forgiveness of sins; except that they include under the term "justification" a renewal, by which through the Spirit of God we are remade to obedience to the law. Indeed, they so describe the righteousness of the regenerated man that a man once for all reconciled to God through faith in Christ may be reckoned righteous before God by good works and be accepted by the merits of them' (3.14.11). One does not have to include 'renewal' 'under the term "justification"' in order to affirm the necessity of works, obedience and faithfulness in the Christian life.

[32] Ibid. 3.14.9.

[33] Ibid. 3.14.13.

[34] Interestingly, although Scott Hafemann (n.d.: 10.8) does not believe that the 'active obedience' of Christ is exegetically warranted, he nonetheless writes, 'Jesus is the functionally perfect image of God, meaning that Jesus always trusts God in every circumstance, as he learned obedience through what he suffered.' Is not this, in effect, 'active obedience' (if indeed 'every circumstance' includes every circumstance of his whole life)?

to speak also of imputation. Stating it somewhat differently, Norman Shepherd affirms imputation, but concludes that one need not affirm the imputation of Christ's active righteousness. For example, in a chapter responding to Clark, Shepherd works through his case for affirming the *passive* (in the sense of 'suffering') obedience of Christ while denying the necessity of the *active* obedience of Christ for a biblical understanding of justification. Shepherd's position can be seen in the following: 'The obedience imputed to us in our justification is the righteousness of Christ that absolves us from our sin, and the righteousness that absolves us from our sin is his passive obedience, not his active obedience.'[35] Shepherd summarizes Calvin's position (which appears to be his own) as follows: 'to justify means to remit sins, to absolve from guilt and punishment, to receive into favor, and to pronounce a man just'.[36] As Shepherd sees the problem, by making salvation essentially the doctrine of justification, the place of obedience and works fades from view: 'we tend to subordinate the importance of transformation and renewal in a way that does not reflect the balance of Scripture'.[37]

We can debate whether Calvin, later Reformers and of course Scripture teach the imputation of the active obedience of Christ. Clark is adamant that it is necessary to affirm that the active obedience of Christ is the ground of justification. Shepherd, on the other hand, sees both Calvin and Scripture affirming that the death of Christ – Christ's 'passive obedience' – is the ground of justification. Let us leave that debate aside for a moment. Undoubtedly, the Son obeyed the Father throughout his earthly life, and this obedience is seen from Jesus' earliest days to his death on the cross – an obedient death. And, this is the key, the life of Christ is echoed or reproduced in the lives of those who have been justified by faith alone in union with Christ. That is, even if the debate over how to relate justification to Christ's active obedience continues, it is clear that Jesus is the one who obeys the Father through-out his life. And this obedience is formed in the lives of those who through faith alone are united with Christ and are justified.[38]

Perhaps the best way to approach this is to observe the unity of the righteousness of Christ: we receive his righteousness and are justified

[35] Shepherd 2007: 252.

[36] Ibid. 260.

[37] Ibid. 273.

[38] As I argue later, it is important to affirm that Jesus' death on the cross was the culmination of a whole life of obedience to the Father. The NT emphasizes the cross as the ground of our justification, but the cross is the culmination of the whole life of Jesus.

by faith alone, apart from works. Christ's righteousness reaches its climax in his death, but of course his death is the climax of his entire life and ministry, and the efficacy of his death is organically linked to the kind of life he lived – a life of perfect obedience to his Father's will.[39]

The role of both passive obedience and active obedience was debated at length at the Westminster Assembly. The Westminster divines chose language on this question that would allow a broader spectrum of persons to affirm the final document. Language was chosen that affirmed the necessity of the righteousness of Christ being imputed to the one who exercises faith. But they were ambiguous concerning whether this was technically both 'active obedience' and 'passive obedience'. Interestingly, some of those who wished to exclude Christ's 'active obedience' as necessary for justification suggested that an affirmation of that necessity would lead to anti-nomianism. That is, they believed that if one said Christ had obeyed the Father fully in our place and such an 'active obedience' were attributed to believers, this would lead to antinomianism. Robert Letham summarizes these participants at the Westminster Assembly: 'if Christ obeyed the law perfectly for us, there would be no need for us to obey it ourselves'; 'if Christ obeyed the law in our stead, we are not bound to obey it'.[40] Nonetheless, in the end the Westminster divines chose to *avoid* the terms 'active obedience' and 'passive obedience', choosing instead to speak of Christ's 'perfect obedience': such language appears to have been a compromise, in order to allow as many participants as possible to affirm the final product.[41]

Now let us return to the main point: by faith alone, apart from works, the righteousness of Christ is imputed to us. The biblical emphasis or pattern (when speaking about justification) is the death of Christ, rather than his life leading up to his death. Thus it is under-standable that a number of folks (a minority) at the Westminster Assembly desired to emphasize the 'passive obedience' rather than the 'active obedience'. But few would want to drive a hard and fast divide between the death of Christ and his perfect life (leading up to

---

[39] This idea is not new at all, of course. Muller writes, 'Since the Protestant Scholas-tics are adamant that the *obedientia Christi* was totally soteriological in purpose, they often refer to it as a single obedience with two aspects rather than as an *obedientia activa* and an *obedientia passiva*. Thus the *obedientia Christi* is both an *actio passiva*, a passive action, and a *passio activa*, an active passion. *Actio passiva* refers to Christ's subjection to the law, while *passio activa* refers to the real obedience of his life and death' (1985: 205–206).

[40] Letham 2009: 256, 259.

[41] Ibid. 261–262.

his death), a perfect life that constitutes the perfect nature of the sacrifice made on the cross. In short, there is no perfect sacrifice without a perfect life. Thus I affirm that in justification we are justified by faith alone apart from works, and that the biblical pattern is the death/blood of Christ, but that this death is the culmination of a life of perfect obedience to the Father (Heb. 2:10; 4:15; 5:9; 7:27–28). As John Piper has written, 'the final obedience of Christ in his death is sufficient to justify his people *as the climax of a sinless life*'.[42]

Conclusion

In this chapter I have argued that a proper understanding of the atoning work of Christ is essential for grasping the centrality of works, obedience and faithfulness in the life of the Christian. It is beyond question that our forgiveness is grounded in the work of Jesus Christ. I have argued that his work is also the ground of human transformation (including works, obedience and faithfulness). When we look at a number of New Testament atonement passages, a clear pattern emerges: the transformation of God's people over time is grounded in the death of Christ. Jesus died that sinners might be forgiven. But there is a 'bigger' design at work: in dying for sinners, he poured out his life and set in motion the cleansing and transformation of the bride who will one day be presented to him. It is not necessary to compromise the doctrine of justification to make this kind of claim. If we are able to avoid reductionist thinking and false dichotomies, we can with full confidence affirm both a traditional or Protestant doctrine of justification and that the cross unleashes a power that leads to the transformation of God's people (a transformation that includes the manifestation of works, obedience and faithfulness). Along these lines Christ's righteousness inextricably and efficaciously leads to our righteousness. Our works, obedience and faithfulness flow from his work on our behalf; so we remain in need of our perfect and faithful priest. But at the same time, what Christ has done *for* us leads to a change *in* us, which includes the manifestation of works, obedience and faithfulness.

For some scholars, one of the central New Testament truths is the union of the believer with Christ. Indeed, for some, union with Christ is the true heart of Paul's theology. We look next at the important reality of our union with Christ.

---

[42] Piper 2007: 213; emphasis original.

Chapter Five

Union with Christ and its relationship to works, obedience and faithfulness

The nub of the issue, as seen in Berkouwer's quote near the beginning of this book is, if Christ has really 'paid it all', how do we speak of our works, obedience and faithfulness in a meaningful way? 'One who has pondered the far-reaching significance of the "sola-fide" doctrine – justification by faith alone – is immediately faced with the question of whether this cardinal concept does not make all further discussion superfluous.'[1] While I a sympathize with Berkouwer's concern, I want to suggest that when one thinks in a historical-redemptive way across the canon, and seeks to understand the nature of works, obedience and faithfulness in the new covenant in their proper context – and their proper and necessary relation to the reality of *sola fide* – a coherent and meaningful theology of works, obedience and faithfulness can be found.

One of the key Pauline insights that helps us think through this issue would be the notion of union with Christ. We are so united with him – and again, this union is effected by faith alone, apart from works – that our lives are for ever shaped by this union: we are changed by being in union with Christ. Thus, when Galatians 4:19 speaks of Christ being 'formed in' the believer, we should keep in mind the faith-alone nature of the 'union with Christ', but should also affirm that Christ being formed in us means some sort of real change in the believer. We are in some way being conformed to the image of Christ over time. Luther put it this way: this 'second' kind of righteousness, where we are being changed over time, must be seen in relation to the 'first' kind of righteousness – that 'alien righteousness' we receive by faith alone. Thus, Luther writes, 'This righteousness [the second kind: transformation over time] is the product of the righteousness of the first type, actually its fruit and consequence'

[1] Berkouwer 1952: 17.

(Luther then refers to Gal. 5:22, the 'fruit of the Spirit').[2] Similarly, Luther writes:

> This righteousness [Christ's imputed righteousness] is primary; it is the basis, the cause, the source of all our own actual righteousness. For this is the righteousness given in place of the original righteousness lost in Adam. It accomplishes the same as that original righteousness would have accomplished; rather, it accomplishes more.[3]

Let us now turn to the key biblical texts.

Key biblical texts

Romans 6

Romans 6 is one of the most important passages when thinking through union with Christ.[4] For Paul, when we were 'baptized into Christ' we were 'baptized into his death' (v. 3). Christ has been put to death and has been raised up, and the Christian has been put to death and has been raised up (6:4). There is some sort of real (if analogous) relationship between Christ's death and my being put to death. There is also some sort of real (if analogous) relationship between Christ's resurrection and my being raised to new life. We have been united with Christ both in his death and in a 'resurrection like his' (6:5). Christ's death also means that our 'old self' has been crucified 'in order that the body of sin might be brought to nothing, so that we would no longer be enslaved to sin' (6:6). Note: the death of Christ occurred so that we would no longer be slaves to sin. The death of Christ is certainly a judicial act with radically transformative results. We need not merge the legal and the transformative, but dare not sequester them from one another, for they are part of a harmonious whole in Paul's thought. Paul circles around in 6:8–11, repeating his same basic premises from 6:1–7. He then carries on with imperatives in 6:12–13 on living holy lives, capping off this section with the reminder that 'you are not under law but under grace' (6:14).

---

[2] Luther 1962: 89.
[3] Ibid. 88.
[4] Parts of Rom. 6 could also have been treated in chapter 3 above, where I deal with the atonement. The link between atonement and union with Christ is to be expected!

Paul states in Romans 6:17 that his readers in Rome have become 'obedient from the heart to the standard of teaching to which you were committed'. He then adds that 'having been set free from sin', these Christians 'have become slaves of righteousness' (6:18). When Paul speaks of becoming 'obedient from the heart to the standard of teaching', it is difficult not to recall other key texts: for example, 1 Timothy 1:10, where Paul lists a number of sins that are 'contrary to sound doctrine'; 1 Timothy 6:3, where Paul speaks of 'the teaching that accords with godliness'; Titus 1:1, 'the truth, which accords with godliness'. These passages do not necessarily draw a *causal* connection between sound doctrine or Christian teaching, and obedience or holy living. But there is certainly, for Paul, some kind of positive connection. And when read in the light of other texts that root our transformation in the cross of Christ, it makes sense to see sound doctrine or Christian teaching as contributing positively to the moral transformation of Christians. As David Peterson suggests, 'the gospel about Christ crucified and resurrected is the teaching that forms or moulds Christian character and behaviour'.[5]

David Peterson later comments on Romans 12:1–2 ('be not conformed . . .'), 'As we allow ourselves to be moulded by the norms and patterns of "the age to come", we exhibit to the world the certainty and the character of the coming order that has already been manifested in Jesus Christ our Lord (cf. Col. 3:1–4).'[6] Indeed, Christ is being formed in believers, and our lives reflect his – however imperfectly and incompletely.

1 Corinthians 15:20–23

One of the classic texts dealing with the First and Second Adam is 1 Corinthians 15:20–23. In what is primarily a passage about the primacy of the resurrection, Paul draws a parallel between Adam and Christ. Death came through one man, Adam, and life has come through one man, Christ. Christ is the 'firstfruits' of all those who 'belong to Christ' (15:23), and all those who belong to Christ shall be 'made alive' (*zōopoiēthēsontai*; 15:22). When one grasps the centrality of union with Christ, Paul's dire words of 1 Corinthians 15:12–19 make sense. Why is it that if Christ is not raised, then one's faith is in vain? Since Christ is the head of the church, we can say something like this: where the head goes, the body follows. Christ

---

[5] Peterson 2012: 153–154.
[6] Ibid. 151.

has already been raised up. The Christian, in one sense, has *already* been raised up, in that the Christian was made alive 'with Christ' (Eph. 2:5, as well as key passages discussed in this chapter, but also 1 Peter 1:3, where God has 'caused us to be born again to a living hope *through* the resurrection of Jesus Christ from the dead'). It is also the case that there is a *future* component to being raised up. Not only were we raised up at the inauguration of our salvation, but we see in 1 Corinthians 15:22–23 that there is a future resurrection for those who are in Christ. Our identity and destiny as Christians are so tied up with Christ's identity and destiny that if he has not been raised, then neither (1) have we been raised up (in the 'initial' sense of the beginning of our salvation), nor (2) will there be any 'final' raising up at the last day.

Ephesians 2:5–7

One of Paul's most dramatic portrayals of 'union with Christ' is seen in Ephesians 2:5–7. Here Paul writes that 'even when we were dead in our trespasses', God 'made us alive together with Christ' (*synezō-opoiēsen tō Christō*; 2:5). This salvation is by grace, and God has 'raised us up with him [*synēgeiren*] and seated us with him in the heavenly places in Christ Jesus [*en Christō Iēsou*]' (2:6). This has been done 'so that in the coming ages he might show the immeasurable riches of his grace in kindness toward us in Christ Jesus [*en Christō Iēsou*]' (2:7).

O'Brien is on the mark when he writes, 'What God has accomplished in Christ he has also accomplished for believers.'[7] Indeed, 'the relationship with Christ that is in view involves their sharing in his destiny'.[8] And O'Brien helpfully highlights what has emerged in my mind throughout this study: to understand properly how works, obedience and faithfulness function in the New Testament, one has to interpret the place and purpose of works against the proper theological backdrop – the glory of God. This is clear when we see why God has raised us up with Christ and seated us in the heavenly places in Christ Jesus. God has made us alive and raised us up and seated us with him in Christ Jesus, 'so that in the coming ages he might show the immeasurable riches of his grace in kindness towards us in Christ Jesus' (2:7). God has saved sinners by grace (2:8), and not as a result of works, in order that no one may boast (2:9). This salvation by grace

---

[7] O'Brien 1999: 166–167.
[8] Ibid. 167.

has occurred 'because' (*gar*; 2:10; my tr.) 'we are his workmanship, created in Christ Jesus for good works, which God prepared beforehand, that we should walk in them'. Good works are ordained by God. Such works are a means to advance or display his glory. This is consistent with what Paul has already argued in this letter. God chose us 'in him before the foundation of the world, that we should be holy and blameless before him' (1:4). God's purposes have been 'to the praise of his glorious grace' (1:6). God's purpose is that our hoping in Christ might be 'to the praise of his glory' (1:12). In summing up Ephesians 1:3–15, Paul speaks of the purpose of our salvation as 'the praise of his glory' (1:14).

Colossians 2 and 3

In Colossians 2 Paul teaches that believers have been buried with Christ in baptism, and have subsequently – through faith – been raised up with him 'in the powerful working of God' (2:12). Similar to Ephesians 2:5–7, those who were dead have been 'made alive together with him' (2:13). Therefore (*oun*), Paul writes (2:16), believers should not allow themselves to be judged for various food, drink, festival, new moon or Sabbath regulations. Believers have, with Christ (*syn Christō*), died to the 'elemental spirits of the world' (2:20).

Paul continues this train of thought in 3:1–4. If believers have been raised with Christ (and Paul certainly assumes they have been raised), then they should set their minds on things above (3:2). And likewise, believers should 'put to death' a variety of sins: sexual immorality, impurity, passion, evil desire, covetousness (3:5). We 'once walked' in such vices (3:7). Now things are different, and we must put all of them away (3:8–11). Beginning with 3:12 and running through 4:5, Paul continues with numerous admonitions and imperatives. For our purposes we simply note that all of these admonitions and imperatives flow from our being in Christ (and various forms of being 'in him' run throughout the letter: 1:14, 16, 19, 22; 2:3, 6–7, 9–12, 15; 3:20; 4:7, 17). Other grounds or motivations for the imperatives are sprinkled throughout 3:12 – 4:5: we are God's 'chosen ones, holy and beloved' (3:12); the Lord has forgiven us (3:13); we have been called to peace (3:15); the fittingness of obedience (3:18); pleasing the Lord (3:20); to avoid discouraging children (3:21); rewards (3:24); judgment (3:25); the desire to know how to answer a person one is evangelizing (4:5). But none of these grounds or motivations in any way displaces the centrality of union with Christ as the ground or motivation of obedience to the Lord.

Galatians 2:19–20

Paul can write that 'through the law I died to the law' (*egō gar dia nomou nomō apethanon*). This took place so that 'I might live to God' (2:19). In an arresting turn of phrase, Paul teaches in Galatians 2:20 that he has been 'crucified with Christ' (*Christō synestaurōmai*). Now that Paul has been crucified (with Christ), 'the life I now live in the flesh I live by faith in the Son of God, who loved me and gave himself for me' (2:20). For Paul the life he now lives is (1) possible because he has died to the law (2:19), (2) possible because he has been crucified with Christ (2:20), and (3) lived by faith in the Son of God who loved Paul and died for him (2:20).

In one sense it is Christ (and not Paul) who lives (2:20). But in the very same sentence Paul can speak of the life 'I now live' (note again the biblical reality of divine and human agency). For my purposes here, it is important to note that Paul lives a different kind of life now that he has come to Christ. Paul has died to the law, been crucified with Christ, and now lives his life by faith in the Son of God who loved Paul and died for him. Paul's present life is now bound up with being in Christ and is a life that flows from the atonement of Christ. Paul experiences the benefits of the atonement – an atonement that seems to shape his everyday existence.

Galatians 4:19

In Galatians 4:19, Paul speaks of Christ being formed in the Galatians. Paul is in the 'anguish of childbirth until Christ is formed in you!' Since Paul is anticipating something that has not completely come to pass ('*until* Christ is formed in you'), we can say with some confidence that Christ has not been completely formed in the Galatians. Nonetheless, there is no reason to think that this forming is either simply hypothetical or entirely future.

The notion of Christ being formed in the believer is almost assuredly to be seen in relation to being conformed to the image of the Son (2 Cor. 3:18; Rom. 8:29), and the fact that Christ – the 'hope of glory' – is 'in' us (Col. 1:27). Likewise, the idea of Christ being 'formed' in the believer is probably not too far removed from Paul's purposes in Romans 8:10, when he writes that 'if Christ is in you, although the body is dead because of sin, the Spirit is life because of righteousness'. Likewise, if the Spirit is in the believer (the Spirit 'who raised Christ Jesus from the dead'), then God 'will give life to your mortal bodies through his Spirit who dwells in you' (Rom. 8:11).

John Murray asserted decades ago that 'union with Christ' is utterly central to any biblical soteriology. He wrote:

> Nothing is more central or basic than union and communion with Christ. . . . [Union with Christ] underlies every step of the application of redemption. Union with Christ is really the central truth of the whole doctrine of redemption. Union with Christ is really the central truth of the whole doctrine of salvation not only in its application but also in its once-for-all accomplishment in the finished work of Christ. Indeed the whole process of salvation has its origin in one phase of union with Christ and salvation has in view the realization of other phases of union with Christ.[9]

More recently, Todd Billings has written, 'Union with Christ is theological shorthand for the gospel itself – a key image that pulls together numerous motifs in the biblical witness.'[10]

David Peterson argues that the transformation that takes place in the life of the Christian is caused by the transformation of the mind.[11] That is, as the mind is renewed, there is a corresponding transformation of the entire person. And if one turns to Colossians 1:21, one finds a confirmation in Paul's words, for Paul there can speak of the alienation and hostility of the 'mind' (*dianoia*). We (including our minds) have been reconciled 'in his body of flesh by his death'. And God in Christ has done this 'in order to present you holy and blameless and above reproach before him' (Col. 2:22). The goal also requires continuance in the faith: 'if indeed you continue in the faith, stable and steadfast, not shifting from the hope of the gospel that you heard' (Col. 2:23). If I read Paul correctly, the logic runs like this: (1) Christ's atoning work (2) reconciles the mind to God; (3) thus the mind can be renewed (4), leading to transformation, which (5) results in being presented holy, blameless and without reproach to the bridegroom (cf. Eph. 5:25–27). And all of these advance the glory of God.

Gerald Bray concludes that an understanding of what flows from the believer's union with Christ is highly valuable. He says, 'In making our confession, the part of the Holy Spirit is central. It is He who gives us the life of Christ and who dwells in us as the pledge of our redemption in Him.' Bray also writes:

[9] J. Murray 1955: 161.
[10] Billings 2011: 1.
[11] Peterson 1995: 126–133.

The belief that a Christian is seated in heavenly places with Christ Jesus (Eph. 2:6), sharing with Him in the inner life of the Godhead, is the distinctive teaching of Evangelical Christianity. . . . Without pride in our own tradition or prejudice against other forms of Christianity, we must surely proclaim that the experience of a personal relationship with God, sealed by the Spirit in the finished work of the Son from Whom He proceeds, is a deeper and more satisfying faith than any other known to man.[12]

Scott Hafemann summarizes his understanding of these issues. In an essay in which he compares and contrasts Qumran and Paul on key theological issues (particularly the place of the law, the temple and atonement), Hafemann writes:

From Paul's perspective, the coming of the Christ has dramatic consequences for understanding the role of the law within the eschatological community and for the nature of the community itself. In Christ, the people of the new covenant have already become the eschatological temple of God. Their own sacrifices now constitute both the worship of God and the evidence of the presence of his Spirit (Rom. 12:1f.). Having *already* been cleansed and accepted by God as a result of the death of Christ, Christ has 'welcomed' both Jew *and* Gentile (!), weak and strong (!), into the new covenant community 'to the glory of God' (Rom. 15:7, within the context of 14:1 – 15:13).[13]

Hafemann also sees the clear links to Isaiah, Jeremiah and Ezekiel that I have noted above: 'For Paul, the transforming experience of the glory of God in the face of Christ is the beginning of the eschatological fulfillment of the restoration of Israel promised in Isaiah, Jeremiah and Ezekiel, in which God will dwell in the midst of his people.'[14]

Richard Gaffin

Richard Gaffin has spent much of his career writing on the nature and centrality of the resurrection. I will not recount all of his thinking here, but introduce his scholarship because it has much to say to the

[12] Bray 1983: 143.
[13] Hafemann 1997: 188; emphases original.
[14] Ibid. 189.

trajectory of this book, primarily the link Gaffin makes between the resurrection of Christ, the resurrection of believers, and the realities of the changed lives of believers. Richard Gaffin links faith, union with Christ and continued obedience: 'The faith by which sinners are justified, as it unites them to Christ and so secures for them all the benefits of salvation that there are in him, that faith perseveres to the end and in persevering is never alone.'[15] Gaffin, in the same work, also writes, 'a faith that rests in God the Savior is a faith that is restless to do His will'.[16]

Thus, when Gaffin in an earlier article comes to summarize his thinking on 1 Corinthians 15:45, he writes, 'Life in the Spirit has its specific quality as the shared life of the resurrected Christ, in union with him. There is no activity of the Spirit within the believer that is not also the activity of Christ; Christ at work in the church is the Spirit at work.'[17] Gaffin cuts to the heart of the issue when he suggests that there is a 'still-to-be completed side of the Reformation' – a side that in no way seeks to challenge or jettison the key (re-) discovery of *sola fide*. Gaffin is concerned by the tendency of many Protestants to so sequester justification from sanctification that there is a tendency to associate justification with grace and then to associate sanctification with works – legalism slips in through the 'back-door' of a certain theology of sanctification.[18] Rather, suggests Gaffin, 'Sanctification, no less than justification, is God's work.'[19] Gaffin quotes the Heidelberg Catechism: 'in this life even the holiest have only a small beginning'.[20] And then he writes, 'But – and this is the point – that beginning, however small, is an eschatological beginning.'[21]

So here again is my thought: we should continue to affirm imputed righteousness vigorously, and that we need an imputed and perfect righteousness that is ours by faith apart from works. Since Christ is being 'formed in us', we should also speak of the born-again, united-to-Christ-by-faith-apart-from-works Christian as being changed over time. We might say Christ is the capital 'L' Law-keeper, while we, by being in and united to him, are lower-case 'l' law-keepers. Our law-keeping is always incomplete and imperfect, but because Christ, the

[15] Gaffin 2006: 105.
[16] Ibid. 78.
[17] Gaffin 2002: 26.
[18] Ibid. 27–28.
[19] Ibid. 28.
[20] Ibid. (*Heidelberg Catechism*, answer 114).
[21] Ibid.

perfect Law-keeper, is being formed in his people, an echo of that law-keeping is happening, by the power of the Spirit, in God's people.[22]

Greg Beale and the importance of the resurrection

Greg Beale argues persuasively for a clear link between resurrection (and ultimately union with Christ) and Christian living. He writes, 'Such resurrection power [as seen in 2 Cor. 4:7; 12:9; 13:4] demonstrates itself by enabling Christians not to be "crushed" though they are "afflicted," not to "despair" though they are "perplexed," not to be destroyed though they are "struck down" (4:8–9).' Beale continues, 'This is another example of how inaugurated eschatological resurrection conveys not merely analogical truth but rather a reality in which Christians participate and is crucial for practical living because it fuels such living.'[23] Beale also writes that Christians 'really have begun to die to the old cosmos through their identification with Christ's death, and they have begun to live in the new order through their union with his resurrection'.[24]

Beale sees a similar resurrection link in Ephesians: 'Paul says that because of such an identification ("therefore," *oun* [4:25]), people should "lay aside" sins such as falsehood, anger, theft, unwholesome and unedifying speech, and "all bitterness and wrath and anger and clamor and slander" (4:25–31).'[25] Beale sees the human ability to obey God as flowing from being raised-up-creatures. He writes, 'Why is the new creation a basis for being able to follow Paul's commands to live godly? It is because without the resurrection power of the new creation, people are unable to obey God's precepts.' He continues, 'Those who have begun to experience resurrection life and the new creation have the power to obey God.'[26]

Conclusion

An entire chapter has been devoted to the believer's union with Christ because it is one of the keys to unlocking the unity of the Bible in general, and to understanding the place of works, obedience and faithfulness in the new covenant, in particular. One key to

[22] John Piper (2007: 215–225) wrestles with this in his comments on Rom. 8:3–4.
[23] Beale 2011: 267.
[24] Ibid. 268.
[25] Ibid. 280.
[26] Ibid. 280–281.

understanding union with Christ relates to the covenantal. Union with Christ helps us understand how the new covenant links to the other biblical covenants. Most importantly, union with Christ helps us to understand how to come to terms with the nature, purpose and reality of the works, obedience and faithfulness of new covenant members.

John Murray was right when he argued that union with Christ is perhaps *the* key to grasping the nature and unity of the biblical teaching on redemption. It is certainly the key to understanding how one can affirm (1) a traditional Protestant understanding of justification by faith apart from works, and (2) the centrality and necessity of works, obedience and faithfulness in the lives of new covenant believers. Our lives are in a very crucial sense our own. But we truly become 'ourselves' only by being in Christ. The reign and rule of Christ in our lives does not diminish our personality and individuality. Rather, it is only in Christ that any man or woman can become his or her truest self. And we engage in works, obedience and faithfulness only through a faith-alone union with Christ.

Another central issue (or group of issues must be dealt with). When dealing with the importance of works, obedience and faithfulness, one has to come to terms with the issues of the place of works in relation to a future aspect of justification, and judgment according to works. In the next chapter we examine these central issues.

Chapter Six

Justification, judgment and the future

Two important interlocking issues emerge at this point in the study: (1) a future aspect of justification, and (2) judgment according to works. These issues must be faced squarely. First, what is one to make of a future stage of justification? Secondly, is there a place for works in this future aspect of justification? Thirdly, should a distinction be made between some sort of future component of justification and judgment according to works? It is important to note that while a future aspect of justification might (at times) be linked to a future judgment according to works, these two realities are not synonymous.

It is common for Protestants to wrestle with some kind of future component of justification, or even to speak of two justifications. Greg Beale correctly notes, 'it is not uncommon in the Reformed tradition to speak of what has been called variously a "twofold justification", or a past justification by faith and a subsequent justification by works, or a "first justification" and a "second justification"'.[1]

First, this chapter will look at the key biblical texts that relate to future justification, and judgment according to works. Secondly, there will be an engagement with key figures who have spoken to these issues. Thirdly, the chapter will offer some concluding and summative comments, to offer a brief treatment of a biblically warranted position.

Richard Gaffin has (rightly) argued that to understand a biblical soteriology (Gaffin is speaking particularly of Paul) is to understand soteriology against the backdrop of the already–not yet nature of the New Testament. That is, key theological *loci* like justification and sanctification have already–not yet components. As Gaffin sees it, the Reformation has properly affirmed the 'already' aspect of justification. It may be necessary for those in the Reformation tradition to continue to work through the 'already' aspect of *sanctification* and

---

[1] Beale 2011: 505. Beale (ibid. 506, nn. 91–92) references Heinrich Heppe, John Owen, Francis Turretin and Jonathan Edwards. I have addressed Owen, Turretin and Edwards in this book as well.

the 'not yet' aspect of *justification*. Gaffin recognizes the delicate line one walks in trying to make sense of this issue:

> To speak of justification as in any sense 'not yet' appears to take away from its 'already,' definitive character. To view it as in some sense still future seems to threaten its present, absolute finality, to undermine its settled certainty in the life of the Christian. This 'not yet' aspect of justification is at the centre of concern in this chapter.[2]

Nonetheless, as Gaffin affirms, there *is* some kind of future justification, as well as a future judgment according to works. Let us turn now to the key texts that indicate a future justification and/or a future judgment according to works.

Key biblical texts

Romans 2:6

Romans 2:6 is crucial to the notion of future judgment according to works. It is worth noting that Paul, from Romans 1:18–32, has outlined why God's wrath is revealed against 'all ungodliness and unrighteousness of men' (1:18), and has spent the remainder of chapter 1 explicating the culpability of persons for suppressing the knowledge of God, and for the litany of evils that flow from the suppression of the knowledge of God. Hence it is no surprise that he says in 2:1, 'Therefore you have no excuse, O man . . .'. In 2:1–5, Paul presses home the inevitability of God's judgment, especially since his recipients apparently insist on holding others to a moral standard to which they themselves do not adhere. Then, in Romans 2:6–10, Paul writes:

> He will render to each one according to his works [*kata ta erga autou*]: to those who by patience in well-doing seek for glory and honour and immortality, he will give eternal life; but for those who are self-seeking and do not obey the truth, but obey unrighteousness, there will be wrath and fury. There will be tribulation and distress for every human being who does evil, the Jew first and also the Greek, but glory and honour and peace for everyone who does good, the Jew first and also the Greek.

[2] Gaffin 2006: 80.

Here Paul clearly teaches that God 'renders' to each one in accord with his works/deeds (*kata ta erga autou*; 2:6). Paul contrasts the one who 'does evil' (*tou katergazomenou to kakon*) with everyone who 'does good' (*tō ergazomenō to agathon*; 2:9–10). This will be a key text as we seek to come to terms with future judgment, and the role works play in that future judgment. For now two observations are made. First, it will not do to gloss over a passage like this. However one parses the details of future judgment and the role of works, it is unavoidable that works play a role at the final reckoning. Secondly, it is also important to point out that we are not (necessarily) working within the sphere (at least here) of perfect law-keeping, or perfect works. That may be taught elsewhere in Scripture, but it does not appear to be the issue here. Rather, we simply learn that there will be some sort of future reckoning, and this reckoning will take into account the works of persons.

Romans 2:13–16

Romans 2:13–16 is perhaps the *locus classicus* concerning Paul and the necessity of works as related to justification. Paul writes:

> For it is not the hearers of the law who are righteous before God, but the doers of the law who will be justified. For when Gentiles, who do not have the law, by nature do what the law requires, they are a law to themselves, even though they do not have the law. They show that the work of the law is written on their hearts, while their conscience also bears witness, and their conflicting thoughts accuse or even excuse them on that day when, according to my gospel, God judges the secrets of men by Christ Jesus.

Paul here is dealing with the requirement of doing the law (however one ultimately affirms law-doing in a new covenant context). The contrast is – at one level – a simple one: one must not simply *hear* God's law; one must *do* his law. However, Paul does not say that one must keep the law perfectly (at least that is not being taught here). A future aspect or component of justification is in view here. Christians, even if they have already been justified by faith apart from works (in the past), will ultimately be justified (in the future) because they are 'doers of the law'. As attractive (tempting?) as it might be to consider Romans 2:13 as 'hypothetical', that simply will not do.[3]

---

[3] Barth concurs: 'That is why [Paul] can say in plain words and not in any sense hypothetically that only the doers of the Law shall be justified' (1962: II.2, 563).

Douglas Moo seems to have the pulse of the matter when he writes:

> The justification by faith granted the believer in this life is the sufficient cause of those works that God takes into account at the time of the judgment. The initial declaration of the believer's acquittal before the bar of heaven at the time of his justification is infallibly confirmed by the judgment according to works at the last assize.[4]

Moo goes on to say that 'the works that are taken into account in that [future] judgment are the product of justifying faith and not the basis for justification itself'.[5] Paul does not appear to be teaching that if one is going to keep the law one must keep it perfectly. Now, if one were saying, 'I am going to try to keep the law as the grounds of my justification,' then yes indeed one would have to keep it perfectly. However, to say that obedience to God's commands is an essential part of one's destiny is *not* to be forced to affirm the necessity of perfect law-keeping. Note what Paul actually says: 'For it is not the hearers of the law who are righteous before God, but the doers of the law who will be justified.' That is, Paul affirms that if one is a Christian, one will obey God. One has been justified (Rom. 5:1), but there is a future aspect of justification, and obedience to God's commands appears to be central to that future aspect or component of justification. Perfect obedience or law-keeping is not in view here, but the necessity of Christian obedience certainly is.

There is a debate as to whether the Gentiles in Romans 2:14–15 should be considered non-Christian or Christian. If they are non-Christian (what we might call the 'natural law' view), then these, though not having Torah, nonetheless obey (to some degree) the 'law' written on the heart (sometimes called the 'natural law'). If they are Christian Gentiles, then, though not having the law *by nature* (they are not ethnic Jews who would have grown up with the law as part and parcel of their lives), they now, by the power of God's Spirit, obey the law. This doing of the law is a further rebuke to those Jews who have rejected their Messiah, and *ipso facto* have rejected their God.[6] But the thesis of this monograph does not stand or fall by how one interprets the 'Gentiles' of Romans 2:14–15. However, if these Gentiles are in fact Christians who have been moved by God's Spirit to do God's law, this would strengthen my argument.

---

[4] Moo 1991: 177.
[5] Ibid. 144.
[6] Cf. Gathercole 2002a.

Romans 5:1–5

Romans 5:1–5 does not explicitly address a future aspect of justification. Nonetheless, it is worthy of treatment at this point because it certainly does point to the relationship between justification and much of what follows justification.

Paul writes:

> Therefore, since we have been justified by faith, we have peace with God through our Lord Jesus Christ. Through him we have also obtained access by faith into this grace in which we stand, and we rejoice in hope of the glory of God. More than that, we rejoice in our sufferings, knowing that suffering produces endurance, and endurance produces character, and character produces hope, and hope does not put us to shame, because God's love has been poured into our hearts through the Holy Spirit who has been given to us.

Paul argues that we have peace with God through Jesus Christ *now* because we have been justified by faith (5:1). And through Jesus Christ we have obtained access *by faith* 'into this grace in which we stand' (5:2). Note: we currently *stand* in grace, and the access to this standing is by faith. We now rejoice in hope of the glory of God (5:2). Even more, we rejoice in sufferings, knowing that suffering produces endurance (5:3), endurance character, and character hope (5:4). And we know that hope does not put us to shame. Why? Because 'God's love has been poured into our hearts through the Holy Spirit who has been given to us' (5:5).

Paul's logic is worth examining. His common triumvirate of faith, hope and love resurfaces in this text (vv. 2, 5). Faith, hope and love appear to work together, and to be linked for Paul. It is through *faith* that we have been justified. We stand in this grace (by faith), and we rejoice in *hope* – in *hope* of the glory of God. Paul's logic is that suffering leads to endurance, which leads to character, which results in hope. And hope ultimately does not put us to shame, because God's *love* has been poured into our hearts through his Holy Spirit – 'who has been given to us'.

Thus in Romans 5:1–5 Paul is speaking eschatologically (in part), and he does so in a faith, hope or love kind of way. In particular, the reason hope will not disappoint ('hope does not put us to shame') is because God's love has been poured into our hearts. But what does God's love being poured into our hearts have to do with the hope of his glory? It is likely (or at least possible) that when Paul writes of God's love being poured into the hearts of believers, and this through the Holy Spirit, he has central texts like Ezekiel 36 and Jeremiah 31 in mind. It would appear that – for the believer – hope does not put to shame for this reason: God's love has been poured into our hearts through the Holy Spirit. In the light of Ezekiel 36 and Jeremiah 31 (and ancillary texts: Ezek. 11:19–20, et al.), when God places his Spirit in a person God causes that person to walk in his ways and obey his statutes. Thus, since God's people are persons who are marked by Spirit-wrought obedience, the Christian will not be put to shame. We can truly (and confidently!) hope in the glory of God (5:2) because the Christian is one whom God is transforming, and it is a transformation brought about by God's grace, by his Spirit, as his love is poured into the hearts of his people. And note: this is linked with justification by faith. We now stand in grace because we have been justified by faith. Justification by faith apart from works is central to the whole thing. But God does not merely justify and then let us sit. He is creating a people who will be transformed by his Spirit. There is certainly some echo of Deuteronomy 30:6 here: 'And the LORD your God will circumcise your heart and the heart of your offspring, so that you will love the LORD your God with all your heart and with all your soul, that you may live.'

1 Corinthians 4:3–5

This is also an important text, for here Paul clearly speaks both of a future judgment, and uses 'justification' language (4:4 NASB: 'I am not by this acquitted/justified' [*ouk en toutō dedikaiōmai*]). Paul is not aware of anything against himself (v. 4).[7] But this does not mean he is acquitted or justified. Why would he not be acquitted or justified if he believes there is nothing that can be held against him? Paul can write (v. 4), 'It is the Lord who judges me.' That statement by itself does not tell us *when* such a judgment will take place, or has taken place. But in verse 5 Paul warns, 'Therefore do not pronounce *judgment before the time, before the Lord comes*, who *will bring* to light the things now hidden in darkness and *will disclose* the purposes of the heart. *Then* each one *will receive* his commendation from God.' Notice that this judgment is clearly future-oriented. Paul warns against pronouncing judgment 'before the time'. And it is the Lord who *will* (future tense) 'bring to light' and 'disclose' what is necessary. For our purposes

---

[7] He writes in the first part of v. 4, *ouden gar emautō synoida* (For I am not aware of anything against myself).

we simply note that Paul, in speaking of a *future* judgment, is using justification language (the verb *dikaioō*). One can distinguish between future judgment and some kind of future aspect of justification, but one cannot drive a wedge between the two. Beale sees in this passage what he calls 'manifestive justification'. This 'final justification makes visible the justified character "in Christ" that was not visible to unbelieving eyes during the interadvent age'.[8]

2 Corinthians 5:10

In this passage Paul, speaking of 'we' (presumably here all Christians), writes, 'For we must all appear before the judgement seat of Christ, so that each one may receive what is due for what he has done in the body, whether good or evil.' The Christian and non-Christian alike must face the judgment, and all persons will receive their 'due' for what they have done – 'whether good or evil'.

Similar to my comments on Romans 2:6, two brief observations are in order. First, it is inescapable that Christians must face judgment, and that this judgment will be based (at least in part) on what they have done. There is no mention of 'works' here, but Paul does speak of what has been done 'in the body, whether good or evil' – clearly speaking of one's actions (or works). Secondly, Paul does not appear to be speaking (again, here) of the necessity of a perfect obedience to God's law. Nonetheless, future judgment will take into account what we have done in the body – whether good or evil.

Although 2 Corinthians 5:10 does not speak of justification, Beale also sees in this passage a type of 'manifestive justification', as in 1 Corinthians 4:3–5. Beale writes, 'the last judgment for believers, which is according to works, is "reflective of and further attesting their justification that has been openly manifested in their bodily resurrection"'.[9]

James 2

In James 2:21–26 we read:

> Was not Abraham our father justified by works when he offered up his son Isaac on the altar? You see that faith was active along with his works, and faith was completed by his works; and the

---

[8] Beale 2011: 512. Interestingly, Calvin understands Paul to be saying this in 1 Cor. 4:5: 'You do that [make an unwarranted judgment] *before the time* – before it has become manifest who is worthy to be crowned, but the Lord has appointed a day on which he will make it manifest' (1981, 20.2: 157; emphasis original).

[9] Beale 2011: 509; his quotation is from Gaffin 2006: 99–100.

Scripture was fulfilled that says, 'Abraham believed God, and it was counted to him as righteousness' – and he was called a friend of God. You see that a person is justified by works and not by faith alone. And in the same way was not also Rahab the prostitute justified by works when she received the messengers and sent them out by another way? For as the body apart from the spirit is dead, so also faith apart from works is dead.

It is a perennial temptation for the Protestant simply to gloss over this passage. But that will surely not do. If Protestants are truly to be a people of the book, James 2 must be faced squarely. We can begin by confessing that certainly Christians are justified by works and not by faith alone *in whatever way James means that we are justified by works and not by faith alone*. Moo's summary is sound:

> The believer, in himself, will always deserve God's judgment: our conformity to the 'royal law' is never perfect, as it must be (vv. 10–11). But our merciful attitude and actions [good works] will count as evidence of the presence of Christ within us. And it is on the [ultimate] basis of this union with the [resurrected] One who perfectly fulfilled the law for us that we can have confidence for vindication at the judgment.[10]

Dan G. McCartney (largely following Timo Laato) argues that a close look at the book of James reveals that 'James has in the background the promise of Jeremiah 31:31–34 that in the eschatological age the law would be written on the heart (implanted), which constitutes the new covenant (cf. 2 Cor. 3).'[11]

Whatever Paul might mean by 'works' and 'works of the law' (and it certainly is contested), it appears that James uses 'works' simply to mean actions that should flow from faith (2:14–26). It appears that when James says 'a person is justified by works' (*ex ergōn dikaioutai*), he is simply saying that when people express faith by works (because true faith is always a working faith), they are justified. That is, when people obey the Lord, they are justified (vindicated). They are seen as being in the right.[12]

One should not miss the obvious in coming to terms with James. Whatever one makes of various New Testament passages that seem

---

[10] Moo 1985: 99.

[11] McCartney 2009: 273. Cf. Laato 1997.

[12] 'O, it is a living, busy, active might thing, this faith. It is impossible for it not to be doing good works incessantly' (*Luther's Works* 35: 370; quoted in McCartney 2009: 278).

to point to a future judgment according to works and/or a future aspect or component of justification, where works play some role, James seems concerned with a justification by works that occurred in the past (in Abraham's life before any future, final judgment). That is, James is happy to teach that Abraham, when he offered Isaac up, was truly justified by works (2:21). James can teach that 'the Scripture was fulfilled that says, "Abraham believed God, and it was counted to him as righteousness"' (2:23). That is, Abraham's obedience (works) is seen as 'fulfilling' the Scripture (Gen. 15:6), where it is through faith apart from works that he is justified.

Perhaps the best way to hold together what (at first?) appear to be disparate strands would be something like the following. A sinner enters into a saving covenantal relationship with the God of Scripture when, through saving faith, that sinner is brought into union with Christ and justified. The sinner is declared just/righteous (the sinner's verdict at the final judgment is announced in the present). True saving faith is a faith that will work, because true saving faith is a faith that (by definition) trusts in, and leans upon, the God of Scripture. Throughout a Christian's life, God looks upon the Christian's faith-filled works, and says, 'This one is righteous. Through faith apart from works this one entered into a covenantal relationship with me. At the moment of saving faith I declared her just. Now, as she walks by faith – a faith that works – I look at her and again say, "just" or "righteous," for this one continues to exhibit faith, a true faith that manifests in works. These are not works that merit anything with me – how could they! Rather, I look at my children, and, seeing them exhibiting faith-driven works, I say "just" or "righteous" upon them.'

Revelation 20:11–15

Revelation 20:11–15 is very important. At the 'great white throne' judgment certain 'books' are opened (v. 12). Then 'another book' – the 'book of life' – is opened. The dead are judged 'by what was written in the books, according to what they had done' (v. 12). This judgment in verse 12 appears to be for Christian and non-Christian alike, and it is a judgment based on what persons have done. The exact phrase 'according to their works' (*kata ta erga autōn*; my tr.) is repeated in verses 12 and 13.[13] There is no perfect symmetry between the judgment of Christian and of non-Christian at this judgment. While all persons

---

[13] ESV and NIV both translate this phrase 'according to what they had done'. I have translated it 'according to their works' to draw attention to the presence of *erga*, commonly translated as 'works' in the NT.

are judged 'according to their works' (vv. 12–13), the favourable judgment (ultimately) of Christians is rooted in the fact that their name is written in 'another book' – the book of life. But this is not to say that works are superfluous, even in terms of future judgment.

Beale points out that in Revelation 13:8 the fuller title of this 'book of life' is 'the book of life of the Lamb who was slain'.[14] Thus, while there is indeed a judgment 'according to their works', this judgment must not be sequestered from the fact that the ultimate judgment of the Christian is linked to the reality of the death of Jesus – and that the death of Christ secures a favourable judgment for those who are in him. Paradoxically, our future (favourable) judgment is secured through the death of Jesus. Because God has determined that his people are to have their names written in the 'book of life', we can rest assured that we will receive a favourable judgment.

Thus there is not a perfect correspondence at every level concerning the judgment of Christians and that of non-Christians. God's standard of judgment (himself!) does not change, and is used in the judgment of both Christian and non-Christian. Nevertheless, in Revelation 20 (esp. when read in relationship to Rev. 3:5; 13:8; 17:8; 20:5; and 21:27) we see that there is a favourable judgment of the Christian because the Christian's name is written in the book of life. And in turning to Revelation 13:8, where we see that the 'book of life' is the 'book of life *of the Lamb who was slain*', we see that we have our name written in the 'book of life' because the Lamb has died for us. And just as the Lamb has overcome death, so those of us *united to Christ by faith apart from works* ultimately overcome death. Beale correctly concludes, 'any evaluation of their [Christians'] works on the last day can be done only as they are already viewed as identified with the risen Lamb and their works done "in the [risen] Lord"'.[15]

Key historical figures

Having looked at the key biblical texts, let us turn to see what wisdom might be gleaned from some of the key figures in the history of Christian thought. In this section we will briefly look at some older figures: John Calvin, John Owen, Jonathan Edwards and Geerhardus Vos. We will then turn to a few key contemporary scholars: Richard

---

[14] Beale 2011: 350–351.
[15] Ibid. 514. The interpolation '[risen]' is in Beale.

Gaffin, Simon Gathercole and Greg Beale. Before offering some summative comments, we will take an extended look at N. T. Wright on justification.

John Calvin, justification and works

Traditional evangelical theology has (rightly) affirmed the punctiliar and *past tense* nature of justification. We *have been* justified, and because of this justification can now stand in the presence of God. But there is also in the evangelical tradition a thorough wrestling with a future aspect of justification, and a judgment according to works. Given the shadow John Calvin casts over subsequent Protestant theology (including over what today is considered 'biblical theology'), it is appropriate to turn to him for a moment. It is worth noting that this is no inconsequential issue. Calvin warns, 'In the shady cloisters of the schools anyone can easily and readily prattle about the value of works in justifying men. But when we come before the presence of God we must put away such amusements!'[16]

As Calvin outlines his understanding of justification, there are two routes by which one might be justified: by faith or by works. Since no one can be justified by works, the only possible route to justification is justification by faith.[17] And Calvin is adamant that one cannot forge some kind of faith–works amalgam that *together* would justify: 'faith righteousness so differs from works righteousness that when one is established the other has to be overthrown'.[18]

Calvin writes, 'Though works are highly esteemed, they have their value from God's approval rather than from their own worth.'[19] Here are the seeds of what Calvin explicates in following sections of the *Institutes*. Works are of value, *but not in themselves*. Similar to how Augustine could affirm that God 'crowns His own gifts', Calvin proceeds to argue that the value of works lies in God's approval of them. Indeed, in this same section he writes, 'it is from God's beneficence that they are considered worthy both of the name of righteousness and of the reward thereof'.[20] Calvin is more pointed a bit later: 'all human works, if judged according to their own worth, are nothing but filth and defilement'.[21]

---

[16] Calvin 1960: 3.11.1.
[17] Ibid. 3.11.2.
[18] Ibid. 3.11.13.
[19] Ibid. 3.11.20.
[20] Ibid.
[21] Ibid. 3.12.4.

For Calvin, any works produced by the unconverted person spring from a sinful heart, and the works are in fact sins: 'in men not yet truly sanctified works manifesting even the highest splendor are so far away from righteousness before the Lord that they are reckoned sins'.[22] Indeed, 'works please him only when the person has previously found favor in his sight'.[23]

For Calvin, any worth that can be ascribed to our works is linked to a person's relationship to Christ. Thus, 'surely, no works of ours can of themselves render us acceptable and pleasing to God; nor can even the works themselves please him, except to the extent that a man, covered by the righteousness of Christ, pleases God and obtains forgiveness of sins'.[24] Similarly, 'Works can only arouse God's vengeance unless they be sustained by his merciful pardon.'[25] Works are indeed God's gift, and *because* they are gifts from God, they are not to be despised. Calvin quotes Augustine approvingly: 'despise not the works of thy hands; see in me thy work, not mine. For if thou seest mine, thou wilt condemn it. If thou seest thine own, thou wilt crown it. For whatever good works are mine are from thee.'[26]

Like others in the Reformed tradition who followed him, Calvin speaks of works as 'inferior causes' of our salvation, and this is all couched against the theological backdrop of the sovereign grace of God: 'Those whom the Lord has destined by his mercy for the inheritance of eternal life he leads into possession of it, according to his ordinary dispensation, by means of good works.'[27] Calvin is of course well aware that he may be misunderstood at this crucial point, so he writes:

> What goes before in the order of dispensation he calls the cause of what comes after. In this way he sometimes derives eternal life from works, not intending it to be ascribed to them; but because he justifies those whom he has chosen in order at last to glorify them [Rom. 8:30], he makes the prior grace, which is a step to that which follows, as it were the cause. But whenever the true cause is to be assigned, he does not enjoin us to take refuge in works but keeps us solely to the contemplation of his mercy.[28]

[22] Ibid. 3.14.8.
[23] Ibid. 3.14.9.
[24] Ibid. 3.14.13.
[25] Ibid. 3.14.16.
[26] Ibid. 3.14.20. Calvin is quoting Augustine on Ps. 137:18. The translation of Augustine (in Calvin 1960) is from *Nicene and Post-Nicene Fathers*.
[27] Ibid. 3.14.21.
[28] Ibid.

Again, God views and judges our works first as God's gifts to us. Calvin writes, 'Yet because he examines our works according to his tenderness, not his supreme right, he therefore accepts them *as if* they were perfectly pure; and for that reason, although *unmerited*, they are rewarded with infinite benefits, both of the present life and also of the life to come.'[29]

Calvin then makes a fascinating comment:

> For I do not accept the distinction made by learned and otherwise godly men that good works deserve the graces that are conferred upon us in this life, while everlasting salvation is the reward of faith alone. For the Lord almost always lodges in heaven the reward of toil and the crown of battle.[30]

Calvin argues that 'no one is justified by works [cf. Rom. 3:20] – on the contrary, that men are justified without any help from our works. But it is one thing to discuss what value works have of themselves, another, to weigh in what place they are to be held after faith righteousness has been established.'[31] And it is the place of these works 'after faith righteousness has been established' that is my concern in this book.

Calvin asks 'whether God leaves as they were by nature those whom he justifies, changing none of their vices'. He answers, 'This is exceedingly easy to answer: as Christ cannot be torn into parts, so these two which we perceive in him together and conjointly are inseparable – namely, righteousness and sanctification . . .'.[32] Calvin also goes on to say that those 'whom God justifies he also sanctifies'.[33]

What does Calvin say about the place of works in relation to justification? He argues that good works in themselves have little value. Indeed, 'In teaching that all our righteous deeds are foul in God's sight unless these derive a good odor from Christ's innocence, Scripture consistently dissuades us from confidence.'[34] Rather, Calvin labours to draw out the link between saving faith and how works are appraised. Thus he writes, 'the good works done by believers are

---

[29] Ibid. 3.15.4; my emphasis.
[30] Ibid.
[31] Ibid. 3.17.8
[32] Calvin 1851: 3.244; quoted in Lillback 2007: 64.
[33] See Calvin's (1981, 19.2: 135) comments on Rom. 3:21; quoted in ibid. 55.
[34] Calvin 1960: 3.15.16.

accounted righteous, or, what is the same thing, are reckoned as righteous [Rom. 4:22]'.[35]

The same theme keeps resurfacing: one can only make sense of the place of works in the lives of Christians if one *first* maintains the centrality and inviolability of justification by faith alone. So Calvin: 'For unless the justification of faith remains whole and unbroken, the uncleanness of works will be uncovered.'[36] The key for Calvin is that not only is the person justified by faith alone, but his or her actions (or works) are justified by faith alone: 'it is no absurdity that man is so justified by faith that not only is he himself righteous but his works are also accounted righteous above their worth'.[37]

Calvin argues that while his opponents grant a partial righteousness to the believer's works, he grants a perfect righteousness. Calvin writes, 'In this sense we shall concede not only a partial righteousness in works, as our adversaries themselves hold, but also that it is approved by God as if it were whole and perfect.'[38] Calvin summarizes his thinking:

> Therefore, as we ourselves, when we have been engrafted in Christ, are righteous in God's sight because our iniquities are covered by Christ's sinlessness, so our works are righteous and are thus regarded because whatever fault is otherwise in them is buried in Christ's purity, and is not charged to our account. Accordingly, we can deservedly say that by faith alone not only we ourselves but our works as well are justified.[39]

He continues:

> Now if this works righteousness – whatever its character – depends upon faith and free justification, and is effected by this, it ought to be included under faith and be subordinated to it, so to speak, as effect to cause, so far is it from having any right to be raised up either to destroy or becloud justification of faith.[40]

Indeed, 'those works, defiled as well with other transgressions as with their own spots, have no other value except that the Lord

---

[35] Ibid. 3.17.8.
[36] Ibid. 3.17.9.
[37] Ibid.
[38] Ibid. 3.17.10.
[39] Ibid.
[40] Ibid.

extends pardon to both, that is, to bestow free righteousness upon man'.[41]

When dealing with passages that treat 'recompense according to works', Calvin writes:

he receives his own into life by his mercy alone. Yet, since he leads them into possession of it through the grace of good works in order to fulfill his own work in them according to the order that he has laid down, it is no wonder if they are said to be crowned according to their own works, by which they are doubtless prepared to receive the crown of immortality.[42]

This leads Calvin to speak about the purpose of good works. He asserts, 'He wills that we be trained through good works to meditate upon the presentation or fruition, so to speak, of those things which he has promised, and to hasten through them to seek the blessed hope held out to us in heaven.'[43] For Calvin, eternal life (in the ultimate sense) is the 'fruition' of a blessedness we *first* received apart from works.[44] Similarly, he writes that it is appropriate 'if we regard holiness of life to be the way, not indeed that gives access to the glory of the Heavenly Kingdom, but by which those chosen by their God are led to its disclosure'.[45]

Calvin affirms with Augustine (from Augustine's *On Grace and Free Choice*), 'how could there be righteousness unless the grace that "justifies the ungodly" had gone before?' However, Calvin says he wants to add something to Augustine's understanding: 'How could he impute righteousness to our works unless his compassion covered over whatever unrighteousness was in them? And how could he judge them worthy of reward save that he wiped out by his boundless kindness what in them deserves punishment?'[46]

Calvin's comments on key texts in Romans are worthy of attention. Concerning Romans 2:6 ('He will render to each one according to his works'), Calvin writes, 'there is not so much difficulty in this verse, as it is commonly thought'.[47] For Calvin (again in an Augustinian key), it is the case regarding God, 'as he sanctifies those whom he has

[41] Ibid. 3.17.15.
[42] Ibid. 3.18.1.
[43] Ibid. 3.18.3.
[44] Ibid.
[45] Ibid. 4.
[46] Ibid. 3.18.5.
[47] Calvin 1981, 19.2: 89.

previously resolved to glorify, he will also crown their good works, but not on account of any merit . . .'.[48] Indeed, 'for though it declares what reward good works are to have, it does yet by no means show what they are worth, or what price is due to them. . . . [I]t is an absurd inference, to deduce merit from reward'.[49] Calvin's logic is critically important. There can be a (proper!) 'crowning' of good works, *without* having to smuggle 'merit' into the equation.

With Calvin there is a sense in which *works themselves* are justified. That is, God looks at the believer's works, and because they are linked to, or dependent upon, a prior (and more central) justification by faith alone apart from works, such works are declared to be just. For Calvin, works do matter, but he is insistent that God sees a Christian's work in the light of, and linked to, justification by faith alone apart from works. Works do matter at the judgment. But even then, for Calvin (with Augustine), God 'crowns his gifts' in us.

Calvin is able to achieve a coherent theology of works and justification *without in any sense sacrificing justification by faith alone*, because he holds to the primacy of justification by faith alone, and because of his Christocentric approach to the issue (particularly union with Christ).

John Owen and justification

Let us look briefly at the great Puritan expositor John Owen, because he wrote at length on the *transformative* nature of the Christian life (particularly in *Communion with God*), and stated theological concerns about an improper understanding of justification (particularly in his *The Doctrine of Justification by Faith*).[50] Owen argues that justification is ultimately singular and this 'one' justification is final. He argues against what he perceives to be the Roman Catholic view, which affirms two justifications (initial and final). He writes, 'that justification which we have before God, in his sight through Jesus Christ, is but one, and at once full and complete, and this distinction [between two justifications] is a vain and fond invention'.[51] But while we must come to terms with judgment according to works, it is necessary to point out – with Owen – that one can (and should) retain a robust affirmation of *sola fide* and still affirm the necessity of works, obedience and faithfulness. That is, one has to think

---

[48] Ibid. 89–90.
[49] Ibid. 90.
[50] Owen 2006 (see the helpful introductory essay by C. R. Trueman).
[51] Ibid. 158.

through how works, obedience and faithfulness relate to justification. Thus Owen writes:

> whereas the necessity of owning a personal obedience in justified persons, is on all hands absolutely agreed, the seeming difference that is herein, concerns not the substance of the doctrine of justification, but the manner of expressing our conceptions concerning the order of the disposition of God's grace, and our own duty, to edification, wherein I shall use my own liberty, as it is meet others should do theirs.[52]

Owen continues, 'Justification is such a work as is at once completed in all the causes, and the whole effect of it, though not as to the full possession of all that it gives right and title to.'[53] We must make sure and grasp Owen's meaning here. He appears to be saying that while the procuring of justification itself is complete at the cross, the possession of justification (by sinners) is not complete at the cross. What has been accomplished (our justification) must be applied (to the sinner through faith). Owen confirms this interpretation later: 'I do not say that hereupon our justification is complete, but only that the meritorious procuring cause of it was once completed, and is never to be renewed or repeated anymore.'[54] Additionally, while one is justified through faith alone, it can be said that at the point of initial/saving faith, one's justification is not in every sense fully *possessed*.

Then Owen argues that obedience to God is incumbent upon those who have been justified: 'Upon this complete justification, believers are obliged to universal obedience to God.'[55] We continue in our justification by faith alone, but this is a faith that – among other things – works. Owen writes, 'It is true that faith herein, works and acts itself in and by godly sorrow, repentance, humiliation, self-judging, and abhorrence, fervency in prayer and supplications, with an humble waiting for an answer of peace from God, with engagements to renewed obedience.'[56] Indeed, 'So our whole progress in our justified estate in all the degrees of it is ascribed to faith alone.'[57]

[52] Ibid. 162.
[53] Ibid.
[54] Ibid. 163.
[55] Ibid. 164.
[56] Ibid. 167–168.
[57] Ibid. 168.

Owen obviously desires to say that the Christian life *should* (and in some sense *must*) be marked by obedience. At the same time, he also affirms that the path to a continued justified estate is by faith alone. He says:

If this be that which is intended in this position, the continuation of our justification depends on our own obedience and good works, or that our own obedience and good works are the condition of the continuation of our justification, namely, that God indispensably requires good works and obedience in all that are justified, so that a justified estate is inconsistent with the neglect of them; *it is readily granted*, and I shall never contend with any about the way whereby they choose to express the conceptions of their minds.[58]

But to make sure he is not misunderstood, Owen then writes, 'But if it be inquired what it is whereby we immediately concur in a way of duty to the continuation of our justified estate, that is, the pardon of our sins and acceptance with faith with God, we say it is faith alone.'[59] Owen is careful to state that our works have no place in justification, and do not act as causes, means or conditions of continuation in justification: 'All other duties of obedience accompany faith in the continuation of our justified estate, as necessary effects and fruits of it, but not as causes, means, or conditions whereon that effect is suspended.'[60]

Owen is helpful because he repeatedly affirms the necessity of works and obedience but is careful as to how this relates to saving faith and/ or justification. Thus he writes:

That God requires in and by the gospel a sincere obedience of all who believe, to be performed in and by their own persons, though through the aids of grace supplied to them by Jesus Christ. He requires indeed obedience, duties, works of righteousness in and of all persons whatever. . . . But that the works inquired after are necessary to all believers, is granted by all.[61]

He also writes, 'It is likewise granted that believers, from the performance of this obedience, or these works of righteousness, are denominated

---

[58] Ibid. 169; my emphasis.
[59] Ibid.
[60] Ibid. 171.
[61] Ibid. 174.

righteous in the Scripture, and are personally and internally righteous, Lk 1:6; 1 John 3:7.'[62]

Owen is of particular value to us since he regularly engaged in polemical theology with those who would deny or diminish the importance and centrality of justification by faith alone apart from works.[63] The following from Owen captures nicely the heart of his understanding: 'Justification is such a work as is at once completed in all the causes, and the whole effect of it, though not as to the full possession of all that it gives right and title to.'[64] Owen's point appears to be that (1) Christ in his death has fully procured the justification of sinners – there is nothing to be added to the cross; (2) through faith a person is fully justified – completely; (3) the justified are obligated to obey the Lord. Of course, the last affirmation – that the justified are obligated to obey the Lord – can be the trickiest to get right.

Owen is happy to say that the Christian life should be marked by obedience. Those with true faith will indeed exercise themselves in 'godly sorrow, repentance, humiliation for sin . . .'.[65] These duties 'are so far necessary unto the continuation of our justification, as that a justified estate cannot consist with the sins and vices that are opposite to them'.[66] So the Christian life will in fact be marked by real heart-obedience. But Owen is particular in his construal of these things. Thus he makes a distinction between (1) 'upon what the continuation of our justification depends' (faith) and (2) 'what duties are required of us, in the way of obedience' (universal obedience to God).[67] At the same time, Owen grants that he will not take issue with the person who wants to state the issue in the following terms (although such terms appear not to be the way he would desire to say it):

> The continuation of our justification depends on our own obedience and good works, or that our own obedience and good works are the condition of our justification, namely, that God indispensably requires good works and obedience in all that are

---

[62] Ibid.
[63] Trueman is correct when he writes, '[Owen] actually placed a very high priority on the role of good works in the believer's life' (2007: 118).
[64] Owen 2006: 163.
[65] Ibid. 168.
[66] Ibid. 168–169.
[67] Ibid. 169.

justified, so that a justified state is inconsistent with the neglect of them.[68]

As Owen unpacks his argument, he makes a clear distinction between our 'legal righteousness', that righteousness of Christ imputed to us through faith alone, and our 'evangelical righteousness' – our righteousness seen in the good works we do; good works that flow from our legal righteousness. Owen contends along the same lines as my argument here: 'the Lord Christ is as much our evangelical righteousness as he is our legal'.[69] That is, both our 'legal righteousness' and our 'evangelical righteousness' come to us from Christ. 'For our sanctification is an effect or fruit of what he did and suffered for us' (pointing to Eph. 5:25–26 and Titus 2:14).[70]

Like Calvin, Owen sees a close link between the imputation of righteousness to us by faith alone, and how God sees our works as 'righteous'. Owen says it a tad differently: 'He accepts it [our 'personal righteousness'], approves of it, upon the account of free justification of the person, in and by whom it is wrought.'[71]

For our purposes it is essential to see where Owen eventually arrives as he argues. To be 'absolutely' (Owen's term) justified, it must be a legal righteousness we receive by faith apart from works. But that person who has been 'absolutely' justified by faith apart from works must indeed manifest his or her justification through obedience, and *without that obedience such a person will not be justified in the future.* Here is how Owen puts it:

And wherever this inquiry is made, not how a sinner guilty of death and obnoxious to the curse, shall be pardoned, acquitted and justified, which is by the righteousness of Christ alone imputed to him; but how a man that professes evangelical faith, or faith in Christ, shall be tried, judged, and whereon as such he shall be justified, we grant that it is and must be by his own personal sincere obedience.[72]

---

[68] Ibid. Owen chooses his words carefully. While in this statement he affirms that the 'continuation of our justification depends on obedience', and that works are a 'condition' of our justification, on the same page he has written, 'Nor have the best of our duties any other respect to the continuation of our justification, but only as in them we are preserved from those things which are contrary to it, and destructive of it.'

[69] Ibid. 179.

[70] Ibid.

[71] Ibid.

[72] Ibid. 180.

Thus Owen does indeed affirm that at the future judgment the obedience of the Christian is necessary. Indeed, works are a necessary feature of a future aspect of justification. Owen does not argue that this obedience must be perfect, or that there must be some kind of quantifiable amount of obedience. And he is not concerned to understand how imperfect obedience will somehow be considered perfect. Rather, Owen seems satisfied to say that the person who has been reconciled to God, who has been justified by faith alone, will indeed manifest works, and these works play a role in the future component of that person's justification.

Jonathan Edwards and the future aspect of justification

Jonathan Edwards wrestled at some length with the place of obedience or works within a theological framework that affirms justification by faith alone. Edwards of course affirmed the perseverance of the saints, but noted that 'the manner in which it [perseverance] is necessary has not been sufficiently set forth'.[73] Here is how Edwards summarizes the relationship between faith and perseverance (and for Edwards perseverance includes within it real works or obedience):

> Though perseverance is acknowledged by Calvinian divines to be necessary to salvation, yet it seems to me that the manner in which it is necessary has not been sufficiently set forth. 'Tis owned to be necessary as a *sine qua non*; and also is expressed by that, that though it is not that by which we first come to have a title to eternal life, yet it is necessary in order to the actual possession of it, as the way to it; that it is impossible that we should come to it without perseverance, as 'tis impossible for a man to go to a city or town without traveling throughout the road that leads to it. But we are really saved by perseverance, so that salvation has a dependence on perseverance, as that which influences in the affair, so as to render it congruous that we should be saved. Faith is the great condition of salvation; 'tis that BY which we are justified and saved, as 'tis what renders it congruous that we should be looked upon as having a title to salvation. But this faith on which salvation thus depends, and the perseverance that belongs to it, is one thing in it that is really a fundamental ground of the congruity that such a qualification gives to salvation. Faith is that which renders it congruous that we should be accepted to a title to salvation. And

<hr />

[73] Edwards 2000: 353.

it is so on the account of certain properties in, or certain things that belong to, it; and this is one of them, viz. its perseverance.[74]

Edwards is essentially right. Biblically, perseverance is a sine qua non of ultimate salvation. Edwards rightly notes that we do not *first* come to have title to eternal life by perseverance. Nonetheless, perseverance is 'necessary in order to the actual possession of it [ultimate salvation]'. Indeed, perseverance is 'the way to it [ultimate salvation]'. Salvation 'has a dependence on perseverance'. Ultimately, as Edwards sees it, faith is inherently pregnant with good works. For Edwards, justification itself is dependent – in a sense – on perseverance: 'it is impossible that we should come to it [the full and actual possession of eternal life] without perseverance, as 'tis impossible for a man to go to a city or town without traveling throughout the road that leads to it'. Indeed, Edwards can straightforwardly write, 'But we are really saved by perseverance, so that salvation has a dependence on perseverance, as that which influences in the affair, so as to render it congruous that we should be saved.' Perseverance is so essential to ultimate salvation that Edwards can write that without perseverance 'it would not be fit that a sinner should be accepted to salvation'.[75]

Perhaps most provocatively, in relating perseverance to justification, Edwards writes, 'Perseverance indeed comes into consideration even in the justification of a sinner, as one thing on which the fitness of acceptance to life depends.' Edwards continues, 'For though a sinner is justified on his first act of faith, yet even then, in that act of justification, God has respect to perseverance, as being virtually in that first act; and 'tis looked upon as if it were a property of the faith, by which the sinner is then justified.'[76] As Edwards sees it, for justification to be 'congruous', perseverance is a *necessity*. Thus, when God justifies a sinner, God has 'respect to perseverance', for such perseverance is 'in that first act [of faith]', and is seen 'as if it were a property of the faith' by which one is justified.

Why does Edwards attend to the 'congruous' nature of justification? Edwards is – rightly – wrestling with something like the following. When we first exercise faith, God declares us to be righteous, or to have a righteous status. He sees us as righteous. It is also the case that in the *future* we shall be declared righteous. It is inconceivable – on

---

[74] Ibid. 353–354.
[75] Ibid. 354–355.
[76] Ibid. 354.

Edwards's understanding – that someone who has exercised true saving faith would *not* persevere.

Geerhardus Vos, justification and human transformation

Geerhardus Vos (1862–1949) occupied the first chair in biblical theology at Princeton University, and his influence is still felt (appropriately) in the field of biblical theology, especially among evangelicals.[77] In his essay 'The Alleged Legalism in Paul's Doctrine of Justification', Vos gets at the heart of the issue concerning the relationship between a traditional or forensic understanding of justification, and the reality of human transformation. Now, Vos is also trying to explicate how one can affirm a fundamental legal principle (including a 'covenant of works') and still affirm a fundamentally gracious way of salvation for sinners (including forensic justification). This is somewhat different from what is argued in this book, since a 'covenant of works' is not essential to my argument. Nonetheless, Vos's insight is precious. He writes, 'Precisely because human righteousness subserves the revelation of God's glory, its [human righteousness's] external embodiment is essential to its [God's glory's] complete realization.'[78] If I read Vos correctly, he is making this extremely important point: if God's own glory is central to all that he does (which my argument affirms), and if the 'external embodiment' of human righteousness (which includes human works, obedience and faithfulness) subserves the revelation of God's glory, then the 'complete realization' of the revelation of God's glory *requires* true and real human works, obedience and faithfulness.

If one grasps the radically theocentric nature of biblical theology, one can avoid all sorts of unnecessary errors. If one really believes that God is sovereign (and good and holy and majestic), and if one believes that he has chosen to create and redeem sinners, and form them into a true kingdom of priests, a holy nation, who exist to advance and spread the glory of God (*without* denying that being a holy nation and kingdom of priests is *also* the greatest thing such a people could ever desire or want to be!), then of course God is going to rule and work in history such that he forms such a holy nation and royal priesthood who truly manifest his presence in themselves by living lives of God-empowered and God-elicited works, obedience and faithfulness. Vos goes on to write, 'Now it is this supreme thirst for the manifestation of the righteousness of God as an essential

---

[77] Two sources related to the argument in this monograph are particularly helpful: Vos 1952; 1980a.

[78] Vos 1980a: 397.

attribute of His nature, and not a semiconscious revival of Judaistic legalism, that underlies the Pauline doctrine of justification.'[79] Henri Blocher concurs:

> Ultimately, however, the promise to the Servant means that *all* honour will be his. Whatever glory and honour the nations possess will be gathered into the Servant's Jerusalem (Rev. 21:26). Scripture teaches that every good fruit of human work, every fruit of 'common grace', will be saved and treasured up in the kingdom of God: it will all contribute to the universal praise of the Servant's glory.[80]

Key contemporary figures

Richard Gaffin, judgment and justification

Richard Gaffin's *By Faith, Not by Sight: Paul and the Order of Salvation* (2006) wrestles with these same issues. Among other things, Gaffin argues that while justification is essential, it is wiser to put 'union with Christ' at the centre of Paul's theology. Gaffin also engages the vexed questions of judgment according to works and a future aspect of justification.

It is important to get these issues right, and not to miscommunicate on the crucial issue of justification. I do not say here that we are justified by faith plus something else (our works or anything else). Gaffin correctly notes that union with Christ is the key to the issue of justification. Through faith one is brought into union with Christ. As Gaffin notes, 'in union with Christ, the ground of justification is resident either in [a] Christ as distinct from the believer, in [b] the bond between Christ and the believer itself, or in [c] the believer as distinct from Christ'.[81] Gaffin rightly concludes that 'b' tends to gravitate towards 'c', leaving the best option as 'a' (the ground of justification is resident in Christ as distinct from the believer). We are justified by God himself, on the basis of what has been accomplished in and by the Son of God. We are neither justified by our union with Christ, nor by the renewing work of the Holy Spirit in us – although traditional Protestant theology affirms the importance of both union with Christ and the renewing work of the Spirit.

[79] Ibid.
[80] Blocher 1975: 43–44; emphasis original.
[81] Gaffin 2006: 51.

Thus, as Gaffin writes, we are left with one option, which is Paul's option: 'In union with Christ, his righteousness is the ground of my being justified. That is, in my justification his righteousness becomes my righteousness.'[82] Gaffin continues, 'The Christian life is a manifestation, an outworking, of the resurrection life and power of the resurrected Christ, become the "life-giving Spirit" (1 Cor. 15:45).'[83] Following Gaffin, one can affirm that the Christian life is one marked by transformation, *without* arguing that justification per se is a transformative work.[84]

Gaffin writes, 'For Christians, future judgment according to works does not operate according to a different principle than their already having been justified by faith.'[85] He argues:

in that future judgment their obedience, their works, are not the ground or basis. Nor are they (co-) instrumental, a coordinate instrument for appropriating divine approbation as they supplement faith. Rather, they are the essential and manifest criterion of that faith, the integral 'fruits and evidences of a true and lively faith.'[86]

Gaffin distances himself from N. T. Wright, who contends, 'Present justification declares, on the basis of faith, what future justification will affirm publicly (according to [Rom.] 2:14–16 and 8:9–11) on the

---

[82] Ibid.

[83] Ibid. 68.

[84] Gaffin summarizes well one of the underlying concerns of my argument. He notes that it appears that for some persons in the Reformation tradition, there can be a tendency seriously to downplay the importance of a changed life in the present, that is, to emphasize what Christ has done *for* us, and to de-emphasize what Christ (through the Spirit) does *in* us. Gaffin writes, 'The effect of this outlook, whether or not intended, is that sanctification tends to be seen as the response of the believer to salvation, defined in terms of justification. Sanctification is viewed as an expression of gratitude from our side for our justification and the free forgiveness of sins, usually with the accent on the imperfection and inadequacy of such expressions of gratitude. Sometimes there is even the suggestion that while sanctification is highly desirable, and its lack certainly unbecoming and inappropriate, it is not really necessary in the life of the believer, and not really integral to our salvation and an essential part of what it means to be saved from sin.' Paradoxically, as Gaffin sees it, such a sequestration of sanctification from justification *seems* to lead to 'the reintroduction of a refined works principle, more or less divorced from and so in tension with the faith that justifies' (ibid. 76–77).

[85] Ibid. 98.

[86] Ibid. See the scathing review of Gaffin in Karlberg 2007. Karlberg's review would have a better hearing if he toned down the heated rhetoric. Rather than Gaffin's two-stage or two phases of justification, Karlberg argues that we should simply affirm two justifications: one by faith alone, and a future justification according to works (428).

basis of the entire life.'[87] Gaffin appears to say that works are somehow 'required', but to be judged 'according to works' is simply to affirm that works must exist for one to receive a favourable judgment in the future – without making works in any sense the *ground* of our future judgment.

Gaffin also forthrightly affirms a future aspect of justification.[88] He writes, 'a future justification of the Christian at Christ's return, in the resurrection of the body and at the final judgment as we will see, is a "good and necessary consequence," fully consonant with Paul's teaching'.[89] Key for Gaffin is his insistence that Paul's understanding of justification must be seen in the light of 'the already-not yet pattern of his soteriology'.[90] Indeed, just as the believer has been raised up already (in regeneration or conversion), and the believer has yet to be raised up in another, final, sense, so one can say that the believer has been justified (from the moment of saving faith), and has yet to be justified in another, final, sense. As Gaffin notes, 'as believers are already raised with Christ they have been justified; as they are not yet resurrected they are, in some respect, still to be justified'.[91] Indeed, he argues, 'for believers, as death is inalienably penal ("because of sin"), its removal – as the judicial consequence of the reversal of judgment already effected in justification – does not take place all at once but unfolds in two steps, one already realized and one still future'.[92]

Gaffin continues, 'Correlatively, the open or public declaration of that judicial reversal, that manifest declaration attendant on their bodily resurrection and the final judgment, is likewise still future. In that sense, believers are already justified – by faith. But they are yet to be justified – by sight.'[93] Gaffin likewise links the already–not yet aspect of *adoption* to the already–not yet aspect of *justification*. Hence, 'As adoption is both present and future, so too is justification.'[94] Indeed, 'Like our adoption, our justification has still to be made public or openly manifested. We have not yet been "openly acquitted."'[95]

[87] Wright 1997: 129.
[88] Gaffin 2006: 83–100.
[89] Ibid. 83.
[90] Ibid. 84.
[91] Ibid. 86.
[92] Ibid. 88.
[93] Ibid.
[94] Ibid. 92.
[95] Ibid. 93–94.

Rejecting the notion that a judgment according to works is simply hypothetical, Gaffin poses what is a central question for evangelical theology:

> How are we to relate this future judgment according to works, as spelled out in this passage and others, to his clear and emphatic teaching elsewhere that justification, as already pronounced eschatological judgment, is a present reality, received by faith alone and on the basis of the imputed righteousness of God revealed in Christ?[96]

True to form, Gaffin finds the answer in the already–not yet reality of our union with Christ. Echoing Calvin somewhat, Gaffin writes, 'For Christians, future judgment according to works does not operate according to a different principle than their already having been justified by faith.'[97] But has the problem been solved? Gaffin writes, 'The difference is that the final judgment will be the open manifestation of that present justification, their being "openly acquitted" as we have seen.'[98]

Simon Gathercole, judgment and justification according to works

I will not summarize all of Simon Gathercole's perspective, but his overall position is remarkably similar to the thesis argued in this book. Not only does the New Testament not deny a relationship between works and final judgment; Gathercole argues that there *most certainly is* a fundamental and inextricable link between works and final judgment. As Gathercole comments on Mark 10:17–22, 'Obedience to the commandments is the way to inherit eternal life in the age to come. Works are again related to the attainment of an individual, future, eternal life. . . . Jesus does not reject reward theology but reconfigures it as reward for service to himself and the Kingdom.'[99]

And Paul is similar. Gathercole argues that Paul's dialogue partner in Romans 2 believed 'in a final judgment according to works'. Gathercole notes that 'Paul makes no attempt to disagree with this tenet of Second Temple Judaism. Indeed, he cheerfully affirms it.'[100]

---

[96] Ibid. 97–98.
[97] Ibid. 98.
[98] Ibid.
[99] Gathercole 2002b: 124.
[100] Ibid.

For Gathercole, 'a doctrine of final salvation by works is an important feature of other New Testament texts'. Indeed, 'Paul is not a lone, isolated voice either in the texts of the New Testament or in the history of the Early Church; rather, he affirmed the importance of final salvation according to works as part of his theology, and it also has an important place in New Testament theology as a whole.'[101]

Gathercole then argues that works do in fact play a part in final salvation, but he wishes to distinguish between (1) the general first-century Jewish understanding of the role of works in relation to salvation, and (2) Paul's understanding of the role of works in relation to salvation. In short, Gathercole sees a fundamental difference between traditional Jewish perspectives and Paul's perspective concerning the *character* of Christian obedience. What is central for Paul, and what distinguishes his view of works from the common first-century Jewish view, is divine empowerment in the lives of Christians, which brings about works.[102] Thus both first-century Jewish thought and Paul affirm a robust theology of works. The difference is, 'For Paul, however, the obedience of the Church and the Christian is God's action, just as "past" salvation is also God's action.'[103]

Gathercole is eager to argue that for much of first-century Judaism, the pattern was works, leading to justification, leading to boasting. That is, works did indeed (fundamentally?) lead to boasting. As Gathercole sees it, for Paul, the pattern is faith leading to justification leading to works (and *no* grounds for boasting).[104] Gathercole's position is similar to mine, argued here: there is a link between justification and obedience. As Gathercole writes, 'Justification, however, opens up a sphere of new life in which obedience to God *is* possible.'[105] Whereas much of first-century Judaism *did* see Abraham as a commandment keeper who was justified on that basis, Paul sees Abraham differently: 'With Paul, Abraham is justified simply at the

---

[101] Ibid. 131.
[102] Ibid. 132–133.
[103] Ibid. 223. Gathercole is on to something. But the way he states his case may actually hinder his argument. If he intends to say that the sovereign God of the Bible acts in such a way that he efficaciously secures and brings about the obedience of his people, that is well and good. But to say that the obedience of the church is simply *God's action* does not help. Are *Christians* actually obeying? If so, then the presentation of their works at the judgment makes sense. But if it is *God's actions* – and therefore Christians really are *not* obeying – then some sort of judgment according to works would make no sense. We are back at the classic theological issue that continues to resurface in this book: the reality of divine and human agency.
[104] Ibid. 232–251.
[105] Ibid. 239; emphasis original.

point at which he trusted the promise, before he had obeyed any of the commandments.'[106]

Greg Beale on future judgment

Beale affirms – with much of the Reformed tradition – that it is necessary to speak (the terms can vary) of some sort of two-state justification, or twofold justification, or first and second justification.[107] We are justified by faith apart from works when we first believe. Beale calls this 'first' justification. There is also a 'final form of justification' – the justification at the end of the age. Beale argues that 'this final form of justification is not on the same level as the justification by faith in Jesus [this 'initial' justification]. Good works are the badge that vindicates the saints in the sense of declarative proof that they have been truly already justified by Christ.' He continues, 'The good works demonstrate not only the prior true justified status of a person but probably also the injustice of the world's verdict in rejecting such works as a witness to Christ, often resulting in political persecution.' He then writes:

> On the one hand, good works are absolutely necessary at the last eschatological judgment in order to demonstrate and thus vindicate that someone has truly believed in Christ and been justified, with the result that this person is allowed entrance into the eternal kingdom of the new creation. On the other hand, such works do not in and of themselves cause one to gain entrance into the eternal kingdom, but such entrance is granted because these good works are seen as the inevitable external badge of those who have internal justifying faith.[108]

Beale does a fine balancing act describing the way in which (initial) justification is – in a sense – 'incomplete' (it is and it isn't!). As he argues, 'initial justification' can be seen as 'incomplete' 'only in the sense that it is a verdict known only by God and the community of

---

[106] Ibid. 243.
[107] Beale 2011: 505–515. Beale speaks of a final 'manifestive justification': 'We have seen that believers' bodily resurrection is a visible, consummative, end-time manifestation of their end-time, unseen, presently justified status. "Good works" are part of this final "manifestive justification"' (505). Beale correctly notes, 'it is not uncommon in the Reformed tradition to speak of what has been called variously a "twofold justification," or a past justification by faith and a subsequent justification by works, or a "first justification" and a "second justification"' (506).
[108] Ibid. 524.

the faithful, but at the end this verdict will be announced to the whole world'. He continues:

> On the one hand, the making known of the verdict at the end both by God's universal proclamation and by manifestation through resurrection and works completes the earlier announcement of the verdict. On the other hand, someone's right standing before God because of Christ's work is completed at the point of that person's initial faith.[109]

Ultimately, as Beale sees it, both 'initial' justification and 'consummative' justification are essentially linked to union. Both aspects or phases of justification 'are grounded in the believers' union with Christ (both his death and his resurrection), the former coming by faith and the latter through the threefold demonstration of the bodily resurrection, evaluation of works, and public announcement to the cosmos'.[110]

Excursus: N. T. Wright, judgment and justification

N. T. Wright, like many traditional evangelicals, sees a close link between our present justification and judgment according to works and/or a future component of justification. That is, our *present* justification is a declaration *now* of what our verdict will be *then* (in the future). This is not unique to Wright. At a very basic level, this is a rather traditional Protestant way of seeing the issue. Wright notes, 'Justification in the present is based on God's past accomplishment in Christ, and anticipates the future verdict. . . . God vindicates in the present, in advance of the last day, all those who believe in Jesus as Messiah and Lord (Rom. 3.21–31; 4.13–25; 10.9–13).'[111]

In a traditional Reformational understanding of justification, when a sinner believes in Jesus Christ he or she is justified. The sinner is declared to be innocent, as 'not guilty', in God's sight. This is the *present* tense sense of justification. But we know that there is some sort of *future* aspect of justification: we *will be* justified. The *current* verdict of 'not guilty' is the *future* verdict of 'not guilty' given to me in the present. So, there is only one verdict: 'not guilty'. And there is

[109] Ibid. 524–525.
[110] Ibid. 525.
[111] Wright 2001: 8.

– ultimately – *one* justification.[112] To be clear, our present verdict of 'not guilty' *is* the future verdict of 'not guilty'; it is simply the case that the future verdict has been announced already. The Westminster divines, in working through such issues, could speak of a 'state' of justification.[113] The challenge of course is in working out the necessity of works, obedience and faithfulness to this future aspect of justification – and whether or not this future justification is still fundamentally a justification by faith apart from works.

Wright writes, 'This declaration, this vindication, occurs twice. It occurs in the future, as we have seen, on the basis of the entire life a person has led in the power of the Spirit – that is, it occurs on the basis of "works" in Paul's redefined sense.'[114] For Wright, justification 'occurs in the present as *an anticipation of that future verdict*, when someone, responding in believing obedience to the call of the gospel, believes that Jesus is Lord and that God raised him from the dead'.[115] Present justification, through faith, is anticipation of our future verdict (or, when we believe now, our future verdict is brought backwards through time and given to us now).

So Wright is arguing that our future justification, the ultimate (foundational?) justification, is essentially marked by works, and the declaration of this justification is then brought back in time to the present. To be clear, whereas my argument contends that justification is by faith apart from works – and then investigates how works at the end relate to such a 'non-works' scheme, Wright, it appears, starts with *future* justification as the most central (including 'works'), and the reality of *that* (future/works) justification is then brought back from the future and declared now.

Wright is certainly aware of the issues raised in this book.[116] He summarizes well the heart of the thorniest issues:

---

[112] But note, historically Protestants (at least of the Reformed tradition) have at times simply spoken of two justifications.

[113] Westminster Confession of Faith 11.5.

[114] Wright 2006: 258.

[115] Ibid. 260; emphasis original.

[116] Discussing the work of E. P. Sanders, Wright notes, 'The main problem then emerges: if second-temple Judaism, having in theory at least accepted that one was a Jew by God's choice, by election and covenant, then reckoned that one had to perform the works of the law in order to remain a member, to inherit the ultimate blessings of membership, how was that further law-keeping to be understood theologically? What account might one give of it? And this, unfortunately, takes us into deep waters not only of Pauline theology but of a much longer and more complex tradition, namely the question, to which we shall return, of the interplay of divine and human agency at the point of obedience' (2009: 74).

How does one describe the future, coming day of final judgment? How does one account for Paul's repeated statements about that judgment being in accordance with the 'works' that people have done? How does one describe, theologically, the interplay of grace and obedience among those who are already followers of Jesus?[117]

We get a glimpse of Wright's solution to these issues in the following:

> the 'Spirit of his Son' (Galatians 4:6), the 'Spirit of [the Messiah]' (Romans 8:9), is poured out upon the Messiah's people, so that they become in reality what they already are by God's declaration: God's people indeed, his 'children' (Romans 8:12–17; Galatians 4:4–7) within the context replete with overtones of Israel as 'God's son' at the exodus.[118]

Likewise, Wright desires to distinguish between 'the *status* of God's people, prior to anything they do, and the *life they are called to lead* which points forward to the eventual judgment'.[119] Similarly, 'there is, on the one hand, the verdict that is already pronounced, and there is on the other hand, as in Gal. 5:5, the verdict that is still eagerly awaited'.[120]

Wright turns to the key Qumran text 4QMMT, which speaks of 'works of Torah'. He sees 4QMMT as essentially a Qumran example of something Paul himself could very well have said, and indeed did say. For Paul speaks in Philippians 3:6 of 'righteousness under the law' – something he claims to have had when he lists his own pedigree as a true Jew. What is 4QMMT essentially getting at, as Wright sees it? Wright notes, 'The works in question will not *earn* their performers their membership within God's true, eschatological, covenant people; they will *demonstrate* that membership.'[121] There is nothing very controversial about Wright's statement here. The most traditional of Protestant evangelicals would say that works are a type of 'evidence' of true faith, and/or that the future aspect or component of justification is fundamentally 'manifestive' (so Greg Beale). Wright simply says that works 'demonstrate' that we are covenant members. This is

---

[117] Wright 2009: 102.
[118] Ibid. 106–107.
[119] Ibid. 144; emphasis original.
[120] Ibid.
[121] Ibid. 146; emphasis original.

simply, as Wright sees it, '"justification" in the present, anticipating the verdict of the future'.[122] This is rather non-controversial, as far as it goes. The real rub – as I have mentioned – is how to link justification in the present with any sort of future aspect of justification (or future justification).

Traditionally, Protestants have tended to say that through faith alone apart from works we are justified in the present. Thus through faith alone the sinner is declared righteous. *And* this present justification is a type of 'taste' or 'foreshadowing' of our future judgment. There is a time lag between our initial expression of saving faith, including our concomitant justification at that point, and the future aspect of justification. Therefore we will to some degree be different persons at that future justification than we were when we initially expressed faith in Christ, and were justified at that point. Wright is correct that works are of course 'necessary' as part of a real Spirit-empowered life of obedience to God. But which 'direction' does justification work? Although this may not be the best way to come at this question, what I ask is, which of the following is the answer? (1) (The 'traditional' Protestant view) we are justified (initially) by faith apart from works, and in the future will (again) be declared 'just'. In this future aspect of justification, works will be required, but do not serve as the *ground* of our righteous status, and do not serve as the *ground* of the verdict announced. This announced verdict will nonetheless declare a person 'just', and this person who is declared just will have exercised his or her faith in good works. Or (2) (Wright's view, as I understand it) we are justified initially by faith alone apart from works, and will be justified in the future by faith plus works (roughly put!). That is, we are justified (in the future, when we are *really* justified) by faith and our works/obedience, and we are justified in the present by faith alone.

Wright, in his comments on the book of Philippians, gives a helpful summary of his understanding of (initial) justification, growth in holiness and future vindication. He writes, 'this is the final destination, the outworking in actual holiness and then in final vindication, of the status which is already given, in the present and in advance, to faith and to nothing but faith'.[123] In one sense, one could simply reply, 'Of course! We are justified by faith alone when we first believe. No "works" are necessary when we believe. And then, over time, since

[122] Ibid. 147.
[123] Ibid. 152.

God through his Spirit is at work in us, there is a transformation that occurs.' The challenge here is how Wright fits all of this together. If we are declared righteous when we believe, and if there is an 'outworking in actual holiness' over time, does this 'outworking in actual holiness' mean that the status of 'righteous' granted us when we first believe is *matched* over time – in the sense that our obedience over time can truly be called *fully and perfectly righteous* at any point?

My argument being advanced here, contra Wright (as I understand him), is that biblically one should say (1) our transformation flows from what Jesus did on the cross, (2) our transformation is due to the power of God's Holy Spirit at work in us, and (3) even after a life of – potentially – radical change, we will still need the righteousness of Christ if we are to stand before, and dwell with, the triune God of the universe.

Again, Wright offers a helpful summary. We see that for him the key – which I affirm in this book – is union with Christ:

> God vindicated him as his own Son, the Israel-in-person, the Messiah, anticipating at Easter the final vindication of all God's people in their resurrection from the dead. Those who are 'in Christ' share this status, being vindicated already in advance of that final vindication (in other words, in the first place).[124]

Wright summarizes the 'traditional' position, which (as he sees it) is nervous about understanding works as a constitutive part of justification:

> 'justification by faith without works' carries on, as it were, all the way through: in other words, that the only justification the Christian will ever have is because of the merits of the Messiah, clung to by faith, rather than any work, achievement, good deeds, performance of the law or anything else, even if done entirely out of gratitude and in the power of the Spirit.[125]

I have tried to show where – at points – Wright's various proposals are less than fully persuasive. He is nonetheless certainly correct that the various future judgment texts are there: 'they sit there stubbornly, and won't go away'.[126] This is indeed the case: they will not go away.

---

[124] Ibid. 157.
[125] Ibid. 186.
[126] Ibid. 187.

Wright goes on to make a good point: we can speak of the necessity of works without having to speak in terms of *merit*. That is, we can – with Paul – affirm the importance of works without *therefore* making works somehow meritorious, without speaking about 'earning' anything at all.

The key is to step back and look at the 'big picture' of what God is doing in the Bible – and on that general point Wright is absolutely correct. I simply want to offer a different 'big picture' than that offered by Wright. And, perhaps paradoxically, this big picture has always been an essential component of the Reformed tradition Wright at times either wishes to affirm or distance himself from.

Wright's 'big picture' is something like this: God made a covenant with Abraham and Israel, and Jesus the Messiah has come in fulfilment of God's single-plan covenant, in order to put things right.[127] This is fine, in general, as one way of summarizing the basic story line of the Bible. Interestingly, while Wright expends much ink in promoting this understanding of the Bible's story line (and often does so by contrasting it with the supposedly traditional Protestant or Reformed emphasis on 'me and Jesus', 'getting saved', etc.), one need not look long at traditional Reformed theology to see that it is replete with various 'big picture' efforts to summarize the story line of the Bible. That is, whether one looks at Calvin, Owen, Edwards or Barth, one finds a long line of expositors, scholars and pastors who have seen the Bible as a rich story of God's purposes for the whole cosmos – that is, both the human and non-human realms.

One can have all that Wright and others say about the importance and grandeur of human and cosmic transformation within what is called (perhaps unfortunately) the 'old perspective'. Additionally, there is a long tradition of such interpretation and affirmation within the Protestant tradition itself (I am not coming up with anything new here).

Wright notes, 'The point of *future* justification is then explained like this. The verdict of the last day will truly reflect what people have actually done.'[128] Wright at one point says:

---

[127] Wright 2009 frequently summarizes – at varying lengths – the story line of the Bible (31–32, 34–35, 94, 98, 99, 100, 118, 128, 129, 130, 131, 137, 173, 178, 180, 194, 195, 200–201, 206, 207, 224, 250).

[128] Wright 2009: 193; emphasis original. He is concerned to show that God truly has a 'single-plan-through-Israel-for-the-world' – a concern and affirmation I, and virtually any traditional Protestant theologian, would share. Wright's repeated reference to this 'single plan' has caused me to think, 'Where does this plan originate?' Where or when does the 'plan' begin? Wright says, 'the single plan *began with the promises God made*

But if we follow Paul and see justification by faith (as in Romans 3:21 – 4:25) *within the larger framework of his biblical theology of God's covenant with and through Abraham for the world, now fulfilled in Christ*, we will discover that from within that larger, and utterly Pauline, framework there is a straight and easy path to understanding (what is sometimes referred to as) the place of 'works' in the Christian life, without in any way, shape or form compromising the solidity of 'justification by faith' itself.[129]

Earning is not the issue: 'Paul never says that the present moral life of the Christian "earns" final salvation.'[130] Wright is correct that (for Paul) the one who has the Spirit must show some mark of having the Spirit: 'the signs of the Spirit's life must be present: if anyone doesn't have the Spirit of Christ, that person doesn't belong to him (Romans 8:9), and "if you live according to the flesh, you will die' (Romans 8:13)'.[131] Wright continues, '"Justification by faith" is about the *present*, about how you can already tell who the people are

to Abraham . . .' (2009: 202; emphasis original). But this is both true and untrue. If Wright wants to speak of 'plan', then we are in the realm of trying to understand God's eternal purposes, at least if we are attempting any meaningful engagement with a traditional trinitarian doctrine of God (shared by Roman Catholic, Protestant and Orthodox). Here we can begin to discern the fissure between Wright and more 'traditional' Protestant (particularly Reformed) scholars. Wright is in a theological and methodological bind. He speaks of a single 'plan', but when pushed tends to say that the plan 'began' when God called and covenanted with Abraham. In addition, when Wright insists on speaking of the 'righteousness of God' as 'covenant faithfulness', he is, we might say, 'temporalizing' this single plan. Here is the rub: to speak of a single 'plan' pushes one into the realm of the eternal or pre-temporal – at least when speaking of God. But to insist so strongly that the 'righteousness of God' means 'covenant faithfulness' means that God's own righteousness comes into being (it would seem) only when God begins to relate to Abraham. Wright is correct to speak of a single plan. One might say that God's righteousness is *indeed* and *of course* his 'own' righteousness. We would be on good grounds simply to call 'righteousness' one of God's attributes (or maybe an aspect of an attribute). For God to be righteous simply means that he *is* righteous, and has always done and will do what is right – and this is a righteousness he can possess with or without a man (Abraham) to whom he relates. Of course God is going to keep his word – as when he makes covenants with Abraham or anyone else. But Wright appears to bracket consideration of speaking of God's plan as God's *eternal* and *pretemporal* plan, and instead to speak of God's plan as beginning with his relation with Abraham. Part of the tension might be that speaking of God's plan as *eternal* and *pretemporal*, and thinking of his righteousness as linked to such a plan, *would by necessity* force one to construe God's 'righteousness' as preceding his covenant with Abraham, and therefore necessarily being defined as something other than 'covenant faithfulness'.

129 Ibid. 235; emphasis original.
130 Ibid. 237.
131 Ibid.

who will be vindicated on the last day.'[132] Likewise, 'For Paul, a stress on "justification by faith" is always a stress on the *present status of all God's people in anticipation of the final judgment.*'[133]

Wright concludes his book with the following words on present and future justification:

> this law court verdict, implementing God's covenant plan, and all based on Jesus Christ himself, is announced both in the *present*, with the verdict issued on the basis of faith and faith alone, and also in the *future*, on the day when God raises from the dead all those who are already indwelt by the Spirit. The present verdict gives the *assurance that* the future verdict will match it; the Spirit gives the *power through which* that future verdict, when given, will be seen to be in accordance with the life that the believer has then lived.[134]

Does this fully satisfy? The key question is, what does it mean that the future verdict will 'match' the present verdict? If the future verdict will be 'in accordance with the life that the believer has then lived', and if the future verdict will 'match' the present verdict, where does that leave us? If the present verdict is 'not guilty' or 'righteous', will we be – at the future judgment, when we receive a verdict that matches the present verdict – *truly* 'not guilty' or 'righteous'?

Works are necessary in the Christian life. I have no disagreement with Wright on that basic point. And Wright has highlighted the Pauline insight that can bring all of this together: union with Christ. Again, I agree with Wright on the centrality of union with Christ. If Christ is a perpetual priest (Heb. 7:23–25; 9:24–28), and if – with Wright – we should resist the temptation to de-Judaize our theology, perhaps what is ultimately central to our ongoing perseverance and works is found in the perpetual priesthood and intercession of the Messiah. And this is found in that most 'Jewish' of New Testament books, Hebrews. Perhaps we should simply say that at the judgment, persons will be judged in accordance with their works. The Christian is one in whom God has placed his Spirit, and the Spirit moves his people to obey him. Indeed, in the classic new covenant passage Jeremiah 31:31–34 God places his *law* in the hearts of his covenant people. If the standard of judgment at the future judgment is the same

[132] Ibid. 239; emphasis original.
[133] Ibid.; emphasis original.
[134] Ibid. 251; emphases original.

as at present judgment (and how could it not be?), then the verdict of 'innocent' or 'not guilty' must *really mean* 'innocent' or 'not guilty'. And if our present and future verdicts are both construed as being 'in Christ', then there is no reason to compromise anything. We are judged in Christ, and because Christ's righteousness has been imputed to us, we are able to stand in the presence of God at the judgment (which *was indeed* foreshadowed when God pronounced us 'innocent' in the present).

Conclusion

There is no reason for evangelicals to gloss over passages that speak of a judgment according to works and a future aspect or component of justification. It is clear in Scripture that God will render to all according to their works – only the *doers* of the law will be justified (Rom. 2:6, 13). Since Jesus came to fulfil and *not* abolish the law (Matt. 5:17–20), and since in Jeremiah 31:31–34 the *law* will be put within God's people, we should – again – be attuned to thinking through how the law might function in the new covenant era.[135] If Christ is the goal/end (*telos*) of the law (Rom. 10:4), we should be open to thinking through how the law might function in the new covenant, *even if there is a significant transposition of the law following the shift in redemptive history from the Old Testament to the New Testament era.* There is no difficulty at all in wholeheartedly (and without wincing) affirming with Paul that God renders to all according to their works (Rom. 2:6), and that only those who do the law will be justified (Rom. 2:13). If what God is doing in history is forming and redeeming a people who will glorify and praise him for all eternity, and who will be more and more conformed to the image of the Son, then *of course* this group of people will be marked by Spirit-induced obedience. And if one does not play divine and human agency against each other in some sort of theological zero-sum game, then one is able to affirm (1) a traditional evangelical understanding of justification by faith alone, as well as (2) the necessity of works, obedience and faithfulness, and likewise to affirm (3) that there is a future aspect of justification, in which works play a role, and (4) that our works will matter at the judgment.

As both Gaffin and Blocher – in their own ways – have argued, while there appears to be an antithesis between law and gospel in the

---

[135] Cf. the very helpful new work by Rosner 2013.

history of redemption, and reflected in the canon, it is unnecessary and onerous to hold that commands are somehow *fundamentally* antithetical to the gospel – or to grace and faith more generally.[136] Rather, if we are thinking in a history of redemption or whole Bible theology framework, we can say the following: God created all things good, including humans. Humans were good from the beginning, and were supposed to grow in the knowledge and love of God and in deeper relationship with him. This of course has been ruined by sin. But there is no reason to think that God's commands were somehow *fundamentally* onerous or *in fundamental antithesis* to his goodness and love.

After sin, keeping God's commands is indeed extremely difficult. But works and grace are not in fundamental antithesis. Rather, we should say something like the following: Jesus Christ, the Son of God, obeyed his Father. The Son obeyed the Father in every aspect of the Son's existence: the Son obeyed whatever the Father said, and was fully obedient to the Father, even to the point of death. Central to the story line of the Bible is the glorious truth that God is conforming his people to the image of the Son, *and the Son is the one who obeyed the Father*. Hence we are warranted in saying that what God is doing in history is forming a people who are being more and more conformed to the image of the Son (the obedient Son), and as such God is forming a people who – *since they are in union with Christ by faith alone* – are themselves marked by obedience. As Gaffin has written, 'To be in the image of God is, by design, to be found doing his will, to exist before him in trusting and dependent obedience to his commands.' Indeed, 'Doing God's will is endemic to the divine image as originally created in Adam and restored in Christ.'[137] Likewise, Gaffin writes, 'the targeted outcome of the gospel is a life marked by "the obedience of faith," the new creation good works (Eph. 2:10) wrought in believers as attendant expressions of their saving faith'.[138]

There may be a way of surpassing Augustine on this nexus of issues, but he provides insights worth preserving and promulgating. When Augustine teaches that God crowns his own gifts in us, he is on to something. Augustine writes in *Grace and Free Will*, 'To one who thinks that way it is, of course, said with complete truth: God crowns his gifts, not your merits, if your merits come from yourself, not from

---

[136] Gaffin 2006: 100–103; Blocher 2001: 121–123.
[137] Gaffin 2006: 101.
[138] Ibid. 103.

him. For, if your merits come from yourself, they are evil merits which God does not crown, but if they are good, they are God's gifts.'[139] In the same work Augustine writes:

> Where he could have said, and said correctly, 'The wages of righteousness is eternal life', he preferred to say, *But the grace of God is eternal life,* in order that we might understand from this that God brings us to eternal life, not in return for our merits, but out of his mercy. Of him the man of God says to his soul in the psalm, *He crowns you in his pity and mercy* (Ps 103:4). Is not a crown given as recompense for good works? But God produces these good works in good people, for scripture says of him, *For it is God who produces in you both the willing and the action in accord with good will* (Phil 2:13). And this is reason that the psalm says, *He crowns you in his pity and mercy,* for we who receive a crown as our recompense do good works because of his mercy.[140]

Similarly, in one sermon Augustine writes, 'So when God crowns your merits, he is not crowning anything but his own gifts.'[141] So with Augustine – who at this point seems particularly attuned to the overarching witness of holy Scripture – we should continue to confess that even our works *ultimately* are gifts. *We* work, but these works are *ultimately* rooted in God's grace towards us, and are brought about by the work and grace of God.

We must never forget the thoroughgoing importance of union with Christ, and that our future judgment is always bound up with who we are as persons who are 'in Christ' or 'in him' or 'in the Beloved', and so on. Our future is bound up with our union with Christ, and there is no reason somehow to sequester future judgment from our identity in Christ. There is a balance here. *We* will be judged, but we are judged *in Christ.* Our true identity as individuals is not *lost* by being in Christ, but rather *only really comes to be* because we are in Christ. Thus, while we do not somehow cease to be because the most central aspect of our identity is that we are in Christ, we must nonetheless affirm that our future judgment is one that takes place only in terms of our union with Christ. By being in

---

[139] Augustine 1999: 81.
[140] Ibid. 84; emphases original.
[141] Augustine 1994: 201.

Christ, *via faith alone*, all that is Christ's is ours, and thus God will judge us accordingly.[142]

There are a number of important biblical-theological issues that have begged for treatment as the argument of this book has progressed. Particularly important are questions related to Adam and his obedience, Christ's obedience and the believer's subsequent obedience, and the ever-present issue of inaugurated eschatology. We look at these critical issues next.

---

[142] Perhaps this is why the 'book of life' is so important in the judgment of the believer in Rev. 20:11–15. While the dead will be judged 'according to what they had done', the believer is dealt with according to the 'book of life'. I owe thanks to Henri Blocher for opening up this line of thinking to me, in personal correspondence.

Chapter Seven

The reality and necessity of works, obedience and faithfulness

In this chapter I try to bring some various strands together into a coherent whole. I do this by examining several key themes – all of which in various ways have been broached throughout this work. These themes are (1) Adam's headship and the centrality of 'advance' in the history of redemption, (2) Christ's obedience and my obedience, and (3) the issue of inaugurated eschatology.

The headship of Adam

Running throughout this book has been the question of the relationship between covenant and command. We must try to grasp the relationship between God, who relates covenantally to humans, and human response – a response that includes human obedience (and works and faithfulness) to this God. Within the Protestant tradition – particularly in its Reformed stream – the covenant of works has been a theological issue. My argument does not assume that such a covenant exists, at least as it has been explained by many Reformed exegetes and theologians. The question of a 'covenant of works' has divided Reformed folks into various camps. Michael Horton, Meredith Kline, Mark Karlberg and many others see the covenant of works as virtually essential to the gospel (this is particularly true in Kline's and Karlberg's writings). Others have rejected the covenant of works, at least in its traditional form (e.g. William Dumbrell, Daniel Fuller, Scott Hafemann and John Murray).

Adam, obedience and the centrality of advance in the history of redemption

One of the key issues that emerges as one wrestles with covenant, Adam's role and obedience is the question 'What would have happened had Adam obeyed (instead of disobeyed)?' Related to this is the question 'Was creation "perfect" at the beginning? – in the sense that there would be no development of creation, since it was already perfect?' Let us start with the latter question (regarding the 'perfection' of creation). While the original creation, including the first couple, were indeed sinless and without fault, the original creation was not 'perfect' (there would be no advance in creation because it had already reached its 'perfect' state). To clarify: all that God made was good from the very beginning. Adam and Eve were given the stewardship or creation mandate (Gen. 1:26–31). In the light of God's command to Adam to 'work' and 'keep' the garden (Gen. 2:15), man was called to exercise dominion, work and keep the garden in such a way that the garden of Eden (and then presumably working outwards to the whole creation) would be transformed and developed in accord with God's will. Without engaging in too much speculation, then, it seems that Adam and Eve *likewise* would have developed personally as they successfully fulfilled the mandate given them by God.

In the light of the possible development of Adam, Eve and the rest of creation, we have to ask if this obedience and development would have reached some sort of climax or end point. The real issue, though, is, can we say anything meaningful about what would have happened if Adam had obeyed? Would Adam have experienced some sort of 'improvement'? And here is why this is important: if it is possible to discern biblically if Adam had the potential to 'advance' in some way, we would then have some ground for arguing that there could be an 'advance' in the new covenant – *since Christ was the Second Adam who was successful in what he did, while Adam failed in what he did.* As Athanasius wrote, 'Mankind is perfected in Him and restored, as it was made at the beginning, nay, with greater grace.' That is, while there was grace *in the beginning* (before the fall), we are ultimately redeemed through a *greater* grace – mediated through the Second Adam, Jesus.[1]

We noted earlier that Hafemann understands the new covenant as not different or better *qualitatively*. That is, the new covenant is not better in terms of there being 'more' of the Holy Spirit, or there being a more intensive outpouring of the Holy Spirit, or of there being some sort of increased ability to obey God's commands, and so on. But, and here is the key point, if we can detect in the original divine–human relationship a situation where the original man, Adam, would have

---

[1] Athanasius 1952: 385; quoted in Leithart 2011: 112.

through his obedience advanced in his relationship with God (whether in terms of increasing trust, understanding, love, knowledge, discernment and heightened blessings and privileges, etc.), then we would have to say that it is at least possible that there could be some sort of similar 'heightened' state in the new covenant rooted in the obedience of the Second Adam, Jesus.

It is important to note that this garden arrangement or relationship need not be fundamentally defined as a 'covenant of works'. Neither must I say (with Kline) that a legal arrangement came first, because grace (as Kline argues) can make sense only once law has been transgressed. Rather, I am quite happy to say with Hafemann and Blocher that the original creation relationship is a gracious one, where God has created man, given him a home, been a Father to him and provided him with all he needs. Nonetheless, the first Adam did disobey, and this disobedience was by necessity punished, given the reality of God's holiness and justice. I am not advancing a notion of merit here. But it does seem that Adam's obedience or disobedience mattered, and there were necessary consequences upon his disobedience, even if we must be circumspect in speculating about the outcome had Adam obeyed.

Peter O'Brien posits that the new covenant 'is better qualitatively in that it is graven on the human heart, not on tablets of stone (vv. 10–11), and it is a covenant where sins are effectively forgiven (v. 12)'.[2] O'Brien argues that the better nature of the new covenant also lies in God's action efficaciously to bring about what was necessary. O'Brien writes, 'The internalization of the law, that is, obedience from the heart, which was expected under the old covenant, will now be accomplished by God.'[3] That is, obedience from the heart of the believer is something 'accomplished by God'. I understand O'Brien to mean that, in accord with texts like Ezekiel 36:26–28 (which he quotes in this context), it is God who efficaciously acts so as sovereignly and truly to elicit obedience from his covenant people. I am fully confident O'Brien would also say that it is the covenant members themselves who obey – even if they obey because of God's efficacious working in their lives.

Henri Blocher and the creation covenant

Henri Blocher affirms the covenant of works, but contra Kline is happy to speak of grace existing *before* the transgression in the garden.

---

[2] O'Brien 2010: 295.
[3] Ibid. 298.

Kline is quite adamant that the primary relationship between God and man must be *legal* (non-gracious), for it is nonsense to speak of grace existing before transgression. Blocher, however, speaks of the original covenantal relationship between God and man as being fundamentally *gracious* (as do I). Thus Blocher does not speak of humans 'meriting' or 'earning' anything by obeying the original prohibition ('Thou shalt not eat . . .'). Rather, through obedience they *maintain* a relationship established by the grace of God – that is, the relationship that exists between God and humans from creation.

Blocher's position in particular is probably closest to what is being argued in this monograph. There is no *fundamental*, *inherent* or *necessary* conflict between God's graciousness and the necessity of works and obedience and faithfulness. As Blocher (referencing the work of A. T. B. McGowan) has written, 'Yet I fully share not only McGowan's interest in "headship" but also his emphasis on *grace*, in the sense of prevenient, undeserved favour as the main characteristic of the foundational arrangement God provided for his image-creatures.'[4] Blocher concludes that the traditional Reformed tendency to speak of a 'probationary' character misses the mark. There was grace in the beginning, and God had provided what humans needed, what would benefit them most: the presence of God himself. Blocher writes, 'the benefits of the Eden covenant are purely gratuitous; the condition (unfailing ratification of one's image-creature dependence on God) is nothing else than continuation in that grace'.[5] And Blocher captures well the general thesis of this book when he then mentions how to make sense of the 'legal principle', of 'He who does these things shall live in them.' Blocher writes, 'This is no legalism! Life is no reward given after works have been done; it is first a gift of grace. Yet, it is responsibility. The creational covenant establishes the regime of human responsibility *coram Deo* (before God).'[6]

Here we are getting to the heart of the matter. Is the first relationship between God and humans one of law and law-keeping, or is it something else? Some (e.g. Kline and Karlberg) are quite adamant that the first relationship is legal – Adam must pass a probationary (and law-oriented) period by keeping the covenant of works. Blocher, on the other hand, while seeing a 'legal principle' in the garden, first sees a relationship of grace, and it is within this gracious relationship that we are to make sense of obedience. Blocher here – quite

---

[4] Blocher 2006: 255; emphasis original. Cf. McGowan 2005: 182.
[5] Blocher 2006: 258.
[6] Ibid.

intentionally – is trying to offer a revised form of 'covenant theology', and those who read closely will see that his position would move one into a Baptistic understanding of the church. To be clear, Blocher sees the original divine–human relationship in covenantal terms, and affirms that human responsibility is necessary. However, he nonetheless argues that the divine–human relationship in the garden is fundamentally gracious. Adam and Eve already have life, and this life is a gift of grace.[7]

Although Blocher does not *deny* the 'covenant of works', he finds such terminology potentially confusing, and he, like many others, prefers different terminology: for example, a 'creational covenant'. Blocher argues that the original covenantal relationship is not a 'works' system, whereby Adam was to 'merit' or 'earn' life. He already had life. Nonetheless, it *is* the case that Adam had the moral responsibility to obey – there is a 'legal principle' at work, for Adam was commanded to obey. Because he disobeyed, he was banished from the garden. Adam and Eve no longer had access to the tree of life. Blocher contends – successfully in my view – that Adam and Even would have enjoyed eating from the tree of life (it was a tree to which they would, apparently, have enjoyed access, and it was *via* eating regularly that they enjoyed life; there was no sort of 'eat-once-and-benefit-forever' dynamic in place).

This leads us to an important question. What do we lose by not affirming the covenant of works? Or, what is there to gain by affirming the covenant works? To come to the point: Do we lose – as some believe – the very heart of the gospel if we fail to affirm the covenant of works? A number of factors motivate my efforts here. First, Christians should seek to understand exactly what Scripture teaches, and if Scripture teaches a covenant of works, we should affirm such a teaching. Secondly, if a covenant of works exists, and if it is the first reality that governs the divine–human relationship, then it is likely that such a construal will colour how we think about 'works' more generally – *even if we are not aware of how such a construal shapes*

---

[7] For insightful comments on nature and grace in the garden, see Leithart 2011: 100–116. Leithart summarizes Athanasius' understanding of creation as a gracious act (and thus there is *grace* before the fall): 'All created reality is a product of condescension; all existence is a gift of sheer grace' (110; summarizing Athanasius, *Discourses Against the Arians* 3.19). 'There is no hint of extrinsicism here, not a whiff of the idea that grace is alien to human life. Grace is operative as soon as Adam is in the garden. Created existence is originated existence, and thus corruptible and changeable existence; it is also, essentially and necessarily, graced existence' (110; summarizing Athanasius, *Discourses* 1.16; 3.1).

our understanding of works (and obedience and faithfulness in the new covenant). That is, if we approach the Bible with a thoroughgoing 'covenant of works' schema in our head, it seems very likely that we will construe 'works' as something to be consigned to a realm of merit, earning, law, and so on, and will likewise think of *another realm*, that of grace, Christian freedom and liberty, and so on; and in this realm, *works, obedience and faithfulness* will play no (or little?) meaningful part. In short, the theological 'picture' one has in one's head will probably shape *other* theological construals, even if one is not always aware of the ways in which such a theological picture is shaping one's theologizing.

A. T. B. McGowan and headship theology

Recently, A. T. B. McGowan has tried to offer a revision of covenant/federal theology by speaking of 'headship theology' instead of 'covenant theology'. He makes such an argument not to defeat or weaken traditional covenant theology, but rather to reorient and strengthen it. Following somewhat the lead of John Murray (who did not see the need to affirm a covenant of works), McGowan speaks of a 'Messianic Administration', thus turning aside from overemphasis on the covenants and refocusing attention upon Adam and Christ as the two 'heads' of administration. As McGowan sees it, 'This then leaves us free to see the covenant of grace as an overarching theme, rather than as a counterpoint to a covenant of works.'[8]

McGowan's argument colludes nicely with what I am trying to work out in this book. McGowan wants to argue (1) for an 'Adamic Administration' and a 'Messianic Administration', and (2) that there is a priority of *grace* over *law* in terms of God's relationship with Adam. That is, contra Kline, grace defined the divine–human relationship from the beginning. For McGowan, the heart of the Bible is an overarching covenant of grace, where Adam and Christ are 'heads' of administrations, and both of these administrations (Adam's and Christ's) are fundamentally gracious.

While I do not follow McGowan at every point, his thesis is in general agreement with what I am arguing, for in McGowan's construal (as I bring it to bear on my own concerns), the 'works' of the believer are never seen as 'meriting' anything, but are always to be seen against the backdrop of a gracious relationship between God and man

---

[8] McGowan 2005: 179.

(whether in the OT or in the NT). That is, the works, obedience and faithfulness of the believer are components of a gracious relationship between God and humans. Such works, while not the *ground* of our standing with God, are, properly understood, *necessary*.

Adam was required to obey the Lord, just as any person in covenant relationship with God is required to obey. The covenant of the second Adam – that is, the new covenant brought about by Jesus – is certainly a *better* covenant. But it is not better because the new covenant does not require works, obedience and faithfulness. It has been the burden of this book to show that works, obedience and faithfulness are simply parts of the life of faith – whether the life of faith in the Old Testament or New Testament era. It would appear that when the New Testament writers speak of the new covenant being a *better* covenant, its 'betterness' is consistently rooted in the 'better' nature of the priest (Jesus is the best priest), and the nature of the sacrifice (Jesus offers a better sacrifice – himself).

The benefit of my proposal would be the following: (1) It allows us to affirm all that the Bible teaches about the unity of God's redemptive plan throughout history. See here especially Jeremiah 33:14–26, where all of the key biblical covenants seem to rise or fall together; they relate in a concatenated whole. But all such a passage requires is that there be a unity to God's covenantal dealings with humans, not that there be a covenant of grace per se. (2) We remove the problem of trying to relate a/the 'covenant of grace' (for which there is little exegetical support) to the explicit biblical covenants (Noahic, Abrahamic, Mosaic, Davidic, new). Such efforts always (on my reading) seem contrived, for one is trying to fit together a theological schema (the covenant of works versus the covenant of grace) for which there is *not* exegetical support, with key biblical covenants for which there *is* exegetical support. (3) It allows us to give full weight to the 'newness' of the new covenant. I fear that when the new covenant is construed as the latest form of the covenant of grace, one is unable to give full weight to the reality and newness of the new covenant.

Headship and human transformation

Christ's obedience and my obedience

Certain difficulties can be avoided by linking Christ's obedience and the believer's obedience. I began this book by noting the question raised by G. C. Berkouwer: What do we say after we say that Christ has paid it *all*? What we can and should say is that the whole of Christian life is a life *in Christ*, and that we can say *both* (1) that Christ has died in our place and has been raised for my justification (Rom. 4:25; he has paid it all) *and* (2) because Christ is being formed in me (Gal. 4:19), there are real – *if imperfect* – works, obedience and faithfulness in my life. Indeed, since Christ is being formed in me, and since Christ is the one who obeyed the Father perfectly for me, there is a corresponding change within, so that – following my Lord – I am *also* obeying the Father. Again, *my* obedience is imperfect, riddled with sinful motives, woefully inadequate, and so on. But it is real and efficaciously being brought about in me because I, as a member of the new covenant, have had God's Spirit placed in me. And God, through his Spirit, is *causing* me to walk in his ways and keep his statutes (Ezek. 36:26–28).

Christ the obedient one

We need not sacrifice the reality that Christ is my perfect sacrifice who obeys in my place – his substitution includes both his *obedience* to God's commands and his *death* for me. But because Christ has died *for* me, the 'righteous requirement of the law' is being fulfilled *in* me (Rom. 8:4). Thus, while Christ is the capital 'K' covenant-*Keeper*, I am a lower-case 'k' covenant-*keeper*. But my covenant-keeping is (1) always incomplete, riddled with sinful motives, and so on, and is (2) always bound to, and in need of, *Christ's perfect and unfailing covenant-keeping in my place.* Indeed, Jesus himself redeemed us from the curse of the law by becoming a curse for us (Gal. 3:13). Part of what Jesus did in becoming a curse for us was to take the covenant curses (e.g. Deut. 27 – 28) on himself. Thus, again, whatever forgiveness was available to the Old Testament saints (in the Deuteronomy example, the saints living in the days of Moses) was theologically linked to the *coming* ministry of Jesus, who is the *grounds* of forgiveness in both the old and new covenant era. But to link Old Testament forgiveness to a *coming* Messiah seems to push us to recognize a *qualitative* difference between the old covenant and the new. However, it is a *qualitative* difference not linked to a radical law–gospel contrast, but rooted in a certain historical-redemptive trajectory that sees in the ministry of Jesus Christ a certain climax and fulfilment of God's covenantal relationship with Israel and the church.

The key issue to consider here is the ministry of Christ himself, and how to relate his ministry to the other epochs of the biblical canon. That is, the key is the relationship of (1) the new covenant brought about by the life, death and resurrection of Jesus, and (2) the rest of the covenants of the Bible. The option that holds the greatest promise is to say that persons living before the advent of Christ were saved by the grace of God – and ultimately by the gospel itself – but experienced this grace in a proleptic sense. And because Old Testament believers experienced grace in a proleptic sense, it makes sense to affirm that this pre-gospel experience of grace was somewhat limited and preliminary. As Blocher has written, 'Enjoyment in advance could not be full and free, as full and free as it is in the Christian era.'[9]

We may need to flesh this out a bit. The value of Blocher's sketch is that it allows us (1) to say that persons in the Old Testament and New Testament alike were saved by grace and (2) to account for the discontinuity emphases (in reference to old and new covenant) in the Bible, particularly the ways in which the Bible pictures the new covenant as a better covenant. Blocher is essentially following Augustine and Calvin in arguing that all persons throughout the ages are saved by new covenant grace.[10] However, as Blocher notes, we can account for both the already–not yet dynamic in the Bible and the less-than-fully-realized nature of the Old Testament experience of divine grace by affirming that Old Testament believers experienced this grace in a proleptic way – since Christ in fact had not yet come, and hence had not yet been crucified and risen.[11]

At the heart of the question of how to construe the believer's works, obedience or faithfulness is the relationship between the existence and life of the believer and the existence and life of the believer's *head* or *representative*. And it is here that we see how important it is to think through the question of our works, obedience and faithfulness against a larger biblical–theological matrix (i.e. against the backdrop of a whole-Bible theology).

Let us grant that Adam was given a certain moral mandate: 'you shall not eat' (of the tree of the knowledge of good and evil); and if you do eat of this tree, 'you shall surely die'. We have a prohibition and a consequence that will follow if the prohibition is violated. Adam was to obey. Let us bracket for a moment what would have occurred if Adam *had* obeyed (the question of whether he would have inherited

[9] Blocher 2006: 261.
[10] Cf. Moon 2011.
[11] Or, as S. K. Stanley has written, the author of Hebrews 'sees the sacrifice of Christ as having redemptive significance even before its time, and that the redemption of people in all ages depends in some way on [that] sacrifice' (1995: 157; quoted in O'Brien 2010: 340).

eternal life for himself and all of his posterity). This is an important question, but let us leave it aside to focus on what is unquestionable. What is clear in Genesis is that God created the first man (and then the woman) and that Adam and Eve had a commission of some sort. It is clear that (1) they were to obey the Lord (Gen. 2:16–17); (2) they were to 'work' and 'keep' the land (Gen. 2:15); (3) they were to 'be fruitful and multiply' (Gen. 1:28); (4) they were to exercise dominion over the created order and subdue the earth (Gen. 1:26, 28). In short, the first couple was not simply to stare at one another, at the land or at the vegetation, and so on. Adam and Eve were *to do something* with what they had been given. There was a commission of sorts. Whether we should see a 'covenant of works' embedded in this narrative is a separate question, and even if one rejects a covenant of works one cannot reject the notion that Adam was created by God, was ruled by him and had a moral responsibility to and mandate from him. The first couple's obedience was real, necessary and meaningful.

Adam and Eve, as image-bearers, were to represent God to the world, and through their obedience, and through the reproduction of offspring who would likewise obey, there would be a worldwide spread of the glory and knowledge of God. The obedience of Adam, Eve and their offspring was to be a key element in the spread and diffusion of the glory and knowledge of God throughout the whole earth. Full stop. Please note the obvious: *the obedience of Adam and Eve's offspring in this scenario would in no way render the obedience of such offspring superfluous.* Likewise, there is no reason to think that the works, obedience and faithfulness of Christians are super-fluous because Christ has obeyed in our place. Quite the contrary: Christ has obeyed the Father as my representative or head. And because I am truly by faith (alone) united with the Son, the life of the Son is being formed in me. Thus I willingly obey, not to satisfy a 'legal principle' of some sort, but because God's plan has always been to bring glory to himself through the formation of a people who represent him to the world as his image-bearers. That is, I really do obey, and this obedience is necessary, for it is God who is working in me to obey him, for he has placed his Spirit in me, 'causing' me to walk in his ways. This obeying is not done to earn merit, but is necessary because God is fulfilling his plan to form a people who will bring glory to him.

The key element in my schema should be obvious to those who have wrestled with the thorny question of the meaningfulness of human works, obedience and faithfulness. If we construe 'works' primarily as a works-covenant (which has been fulfilled by Jesus), we will probably (possibly?) fail *then* to flesh out meaningfully why the works of the believer really matter. However, if we have a historical-redemptive schema where works, obedience and faithfulness are true human acts (although efficaciously elicited by God), and these acts (works, obedience, faithfulness) are a part of the divine plan whereby God is glorified and humans fulfil their mission to represent God to the world, then we have a biblically faithful and meaningful framework to make sense of works, obedience and faithfulness.

As Greg Beale says in commenting on the ending of Psalm 72 (which for him hearkens back to Gen. 1:26–28), 'the king *and his seed* were to be images of God, bearing his glorious image throughout creation'.[12] Commenting on Psalm 73, Beale notes 'that the individual believers and their behavior are a part of larger patterns of redemptive-historical movements, such as final judgment and reward'.[13] Beale captures the heart of what I am trying to argue:

What happened to Christ in his life, death, and resurrection contains patterns of things that not only recapitulate earlier OT historical patterns but also embody patterns of things that will happen to his people – for example, with respect to his suffering, resurrection as first fruits, his identity as Son of God (Christians are adopted sons/daughters) and Son of Man (i.e., Adam: Christians become true humanity in Christ), being a light to the nations, reception of the Holy Spirit, keeping of the law, restoration or reconciliation to God's presence from death, and his vindication becoming the Christian's justification.[14]

Beale says something similar a little later, when commenting on the great tribulation – and is laying out the relationship of the First Adam (Adam) and the Second Adam (Jesus). Beale writes:

But, unlike the first Adam, the eschatological Adam [Jesus] will withstand the attack and overcome the forces of evil. Likewise, his followers will be subject to this recapitulated tribulation of deception and will also overcome it through their identification with their latter-day leader, who paved the way for them.[15]

[12] Beale 2011: 78; emphasis original.
[13] Ibid.
[14] Ibid. 181.
[15] Ibid. 189.

Exactly. It is because Christ is our head, and because we are united to him by faith that Christians likewise are overcomers or conquerors (Rev. 2). Is it the case that Christ overcomes on our behalf? Yes. Is it also the case that Christians overcome through Christ? Yes. There is no reason to play Christ's conquering for us over against the believer's conquering. We conquer, but we conquer because we are united (by faith alone) to the conqueror – our head and Lord, Jesus Christ.

Likewise, as Beale points out, believers will also reign with Christ: 'Believers are not mere subjects in Christ's kingdom. That John uses the word "fellow partaker" underscores the active involvement of saints, not only in enduring tribulation but also in reigning in the midst of it.'[16] This does not mean in any way that our reign impinges upon Christ's reign. Rather, it is only because of his reign and because believers are united with him by faith that believers reign. Thus, as Beale writes:

> John views Christians as identified corporately with Jesus: their kingly endurance through trial is 'in Jesus'. . . . This corporate identity is the basis for the trials that confront them, as well as for their ability to endure such trials and to participate in the kingdom as kings. If Christ went through the end-time tribulation, so must those who identify with him.[17]

And to draw the obvious inference: it is only because of Christ's obedience and because believers are united with him by faith that believers obey. And our obedience in no way impinges upon or diminishes Christ's obedience. Rather, we obey because we are in Christ – the ultimate obeying one. As Beale, contrasting the first and second Adams, writes, 'the last Adam, Jesus, and his true followers succeed in contrast to the first Adam, who failed and was deceived by the devil'.[18]

Already–not yet: the reality of inaugurated eschatology

William J. Dumbrell is correct: eschatology is the key to understanding the entire Bible.[19] From Genesis to Revelation the heart of things

[16] Ibid. 208.
[17] Ibid.
[18] Ibid. 218.
[19] This is most fully and helpfully explicated by Dumbrell (1994).

is the eschatological nature and structure of the entire canon. This is not to say that the whole Bible is concerned with a particular 'end times' scenario (although, in one sense, as we have seen, it is). It is to say that from the earliest pages of holy writ onward, we see that a forward-looking element is the key to the Scriptures. All Scripture is structured by the fact that there is something to which it is *pointing*. There is a *goal* to which Scripture is moving. The Bible begins in a garden and ends in a garden city. The first Adam is a type of king-priest, and at the end there is a whole *kingdom* of priests that God – over time – has formed. God gives instructions for how to build the first temple, but at the end of all things we see that the Lord God himself and the Lamb are the temple (Rev. 20:22). We could multiply many times such basic examples.

As we move into the New Testament, we discover what is often called an 'already–not yet' principle. The new age or new era is *already* here, but it is *not yet* here in the fullest sense. That is, with the ministry of Jesus, and with his death and resurrection there has been a funda-mental 'advance' or shift in redemptive history. The 'world to come' has arrived, arrived in principle or arrived partially. But there is more yet to come. Vos is often credited with this fundamental insight, and Ladd later developed Vos's schema.[20]

It is impossible to grasp the importance of works, obedience and faithfulness in the Christian life without grasping something of the importance and nature of the 'already–not yet' reality of the New Testament. The Bible teaches that works, obedience and faithfulness are a part of the Christian life. Such works, obedience and faithful-ness are possible only because of what God has accomplished for us in the death, burial, resurrection of Christ, and because of the sub-sequent role of the Spirit in the life of the believer. At the same time, while the believer is a new creation, a new person, she is not as new as she will one day be. While the believer has crossed from death to life (John 5:24), she is still being conformed to the image of the Son (2 Cor. 3:18), and is not as fully transformed and changed as she will be (1 Cor. 13:12). Thus the believer – in terms of her works, obedience and faithfulness – lives in the already–not yet tension at the very heart of the New Testament.

Vos asks exactly the right question. If the future state of the Christian is 'the permanent state of blessedness' (on which virtually all Christians agree), then, 'The principal question is whether the static

---

[20] Cf. Vos 1952 and Ladd 1993: 66–67.

outcome, the permanent state of blessedness predicted, is actually included, sometimes at least, in the "acherith."'[21] That is, should we see aspects of 'the permanent state of blessedness' in the 'last days' – *which have broken into the present because we are living in the 'last days' now*?

And one cannot divorce the New Testament's (esp. Pauline) already–not yet eschatological framework from his conception of being 'in Christ', or 'union with Christ. Thus we see that we are *already* raised up and hidden with Christ *now* (Col. 3:1, 3–4), but yet are nonetheless commanded – in the same passage – to 'set your minds on things that are above' (Col. 3:2). Likewise, in Philippians we read that our commonwealth or citizenship is in heaven (since Christ is there), but we are nonetheless told that we await from *it* (the heaven just mentioned) our Saviour, Jesus Christ (Phil. 3:20). As Vos writes, 'this whole representation of the Christian state as centrally and potentially anchored in heaven is not the abrogation, it is the most intense and the most practical assertion of the other-worldly tenor of the believer's life'.[22] Vos closes the summary of his chapter 'The Structure of the Pauline Eschatology' with these tantalizing words: 'the Christian has only his members upon earth, which are to be mortified; himself, and as a whole, he belongs to the high mountain-land above, Col. 3:5'.[23] Here Vos is pushing in exactly the direction of my argument. Believers truly are 'raised with Christ' (Col. 3:1; cf. Eph. 2:5–6) and 'hidden with Christ in God' (Col. 3:3). Our true citizenship is in heaven (Phil. 3:20). We – in some mysterious sense – are *there*, in heaven. Vos says that only our 'members' are still upon the earth, and our members are to be mortified (we might want to tweak or challenge Vos's exact way of stating this). But Vos is on the right track: we have been raised up with Christ, and in the meantime are to mortify the deeds of the body. But the two truths are *not* simply being stated, without saying anything about the relationship between the two. That is, as Vos sees it Paul affirms that we have been raised up with Christ, and are to mortify the deeds of the body. *And*, as Vos sees it, the reality of being raised up with Christ is the ground or motivation of morti-fying the deeds of the body. And this relationship is inherently bound up with Vos's (Paul's?) already–not yet eschatological structure. As Vos notes, 'the shaping of soteriology by eschatology is not so much

---

[21] Vos 1952: 6. 'Acherith' is Vos's transliteration of the Hebrew word meaning 'last', as in 'last days'. The Hebrew word is *'aḥărît*. See ibid. 1.

[22] Ibid. 39.

[23] Ibid. 41.

in terminology; it proceeds from the *actual realities themselves* and the language simply is adjusted to that'.[24]

As Vos explicates his position, it is important to grasp his understanding of the relationship of eschatology to soteriology. It is important not to construe the already–not yet eschatological structure *simply* in terms of the subjective or internal state of the individual. Vos argues that it is not simply that the believer is a new *creature*. Rather, the Christian lives amid a new *creation*. As Vos writes, 'There has been created a totally new environment, or, more accurately speaking, a totally new world, in which the person spoken of is an inhabitant and participator.'[25] Vos continues, 'It is not in the first place the interiority of the subject that has undergone the change, although that, of course is not to be excluded. The whole surrounding world has assumed a new aspect and complexion.'[26] If the believer is a new creation, and if the believer is living in and amid a 'new creation', does it not make sense to affirm that the believer will manifest this newness with some real – if imperfect – works, obedience and faithfulness?

For Vos, an understanding of Pauline eschatology helps us to grasp that with the in-breaking of the age to come we will experience something of future blessedness in the present. As Vos notes regarding Paul's eschatology, 'the emergence of an idea in which without clear distinction present enjoyment and joyful anticipation of the final deliverance mingle'.[27] Vos goes on to write, 'Paul and his converts by a sort of reversion thought themselves saved as in the future so in the present.'[28] Eschatology is at the heart of soteriology, for as Vos notes, 'the priority belongs in the apostle's mind to the eschatological aspect'. Indeed, 'salvation is spoken of in an absolute way, as though it were the only conception customary'.[29]

Beale argues that the many Old Testament promises of the sending of the Spirit, of the Spirit giving new life and being poured out, and producing obedience in God's people, have all begun in the New Testament. Indeed, the presence of the Spirit can be seen in the ministry of Jesus himself: 'the physical and spiritual curses of the fall are starting to be taken away by Jesus'.[30] And of course it is Jesus, and

[24] Ibid. 46; my emphasis.
[25] Ibid. 47.
[26] Ibid.
[27] Ibid. 51.
[28] Ibid.
[29] Ibid. 53–54.
[30] Beale 2011: 569.

our union with him, that is central. Commenting on John 20:21–23 in relationship to Genesis 2:7 (where God 'breathed' into Adam, making him a living being), Beale writes, 'Jesus is empowering his followers not with physical life, as with Adam, but with spiritual empowerment to do what Adam and others had failed to do.'[31]

Beale's 'creation–new creation' motif is one angle that allows us to affirm the *newness* of the new covenant without positing a radical old–new distinction that makes it difficult to grasp how the Old Testament saints could have been saved. It is because of an advance in redemptive history, an advance that reaches a climax in the person, ministry, death and resurrection of Jesus, that the 'new creation' has broken into history. As Beale writes, 'Just as God's breathing into Adam made him alive and a part of the first creation, so Jesus's breathing into the disciples the Spirit might well be considered an act incorporating them into a stage of new creation, which Jesus had inaugurated already by his resurrection.'[32]

Beale spends many pages arguing for the transformative nature of the work of the Spirit. There is no need to rehearse his entire argument. On the whole I find it convincing. We might simply ask, what does the transformative work of the Holy Spirit look like? Or, applied to my argument in this book, does the Spirit's transformative work entail moving God's people to obey God's word? It would seem that this is clearly the import of Ezekiel 36. For in Ezekiel 36:27 we read, 'And I will put my Spirit within you, and cause you to walk in my statutes and be careful to obey my rules.' That is, at least *one* of the things the Spirit does is efficaciously move his people to obey God. This is not an issue of earning merit, for example. Obeying the Lord is simply a mark of the presence of the Holy Spirit.

But it is the notion of 'advance' or 'development' in the history of redemption I want to emphasize. If the 'last days' began in the first century (Joel 2 and Acts 2), and it is clear that this is the case, then it is appropriate to see that from that time forward believers have been living in the 'last days', and should live lives characterized by the 'last days'. As Beale writes, 'if Christians have begun to be end-time resurrected creatures, then they have resurrection power not to "let sin reign in [their mortal bodies] . . . but present [themselves] to God as those alive from the dead (6:12–13)"'.[33] That is, if we indeed are (and have been) living in the last days, and if the last days are marked by

[31] Ibid. 571–572.
[32] Ibid. 572.
[33] Ibid. 251.

the presence of the Spirit (in a heightened and 'last days' kind of way), then it follows that the Spirit is assuredly present in a particularly powerful way.

Insight from Jonathan Edwards: the all-encompassing nature of the work of redemption

As is the case with any discipline – including theology – one finds that the giants of the field have often wrestled with this or that question which perplexes people in the present. Particularly helpful in thinking through the issues raised in this book is Jonathan Edwards's *A History of the Work of Redemption*, which is a 'sketch' of a larger *magnum opus* Edwards was unable to complete before his death. Nonetheless, at some 350 pages it is no small work, though in Edwards's mind it was simply a sketch of the work he wanted to write. It is a summary of Edwards's 'biblical theology' – at least what today would be called a 'biblical theology'.

What is particularly helpful is how Edwards speaks of the *nature* and *goal* of redemption. Edwards grants that there is both a narrower and a broader way of speaking of redemption. The 'narrow' sense (not being used negatively by Edwards) speaks of 'redemption' in terms of the death, burial and resurrection of Jesus. But in the broader sense, for Edwards the work of 'redemption' concerns all that God has been doing from the act of creation forward. Thus Edwards writes that 'The work of redemption is a work that God carries on from the fall of man to the end of the world.'[34] Indeed, 'For salvation is the sum of all those works of God by which the benefits that are by the covenant of grace are procured and bestowed.'[35] For Edwards it is essential to grasp the unity of the works of creation and redemption. There is not a 'Plan A' and a 'Plan B' in terms of redemption. God's plan was *always* to redeem sinners, and thus creation is linked with redemption. As Edwards writes, 'The creating heaven was in order to the Work of Redemption; it was to be an habitation for the redeemed and the Redeemer.'[36] That is, creation is brought into being *in order to serve* the purpose of redemption. This is not to denigrate the reality, importance or nature of creation. Rather, Edwards's construal points out that *from the very beginning* there was a *telos* or goal/end in creating the world. And a part

[34] Edwards 1989: 116.
[35] Ibid. 115.
[36] Ibid. 118.

of this goal was that creation should serve as a 'habitation' for the redeemed. And that goal (creation serving as a habitation for the redeemed) would in turn serve the more ultimate goal of the glory of God.

To cut to the chase: when we, taking a cue from Edwards, begin to understand redemption in this larger and broader sense (from the creation of the world forward), we will see human transformation (including works, obedience and faithfulness) as a constitutive part of God's redemptive plan, and not a peripheral or optional 'addition' to his plan. God, as Edwards sees it, is building a temple, forming a people. It is certainly appropriate also to speak of redemption in the more particular sense of the forgiveness of sins brought about by Jesus' death, burial and resurrection. But the work of redemption must be seen in relation to God's revealed plan and will – which includes the transformation of sinners (including real, though imperfect, works, obedience and faithfulness). Hence Edwards writes:

> The Work of Redemption with respect to the grand design in general as it relates to the universal subject and end of it, is carried on from the fall of man to the end of the world in a different manner, not merely by the repeating and renewing the same effect on the different subjects of it, but by many successive works and dispensations of God, all tending to one great end and effect, all united as the several parts of a scheme, and altogether making up one great work. Like an house or temple that is building, first the workmen are sent forth, then the materials are gathered, then the ground fitted, then the foundation is laid, then the superstructure erected one part after another, till at length the topstone is laid. And all is finished. Now the Work of Redemption in that large sense that has been explained may be compared to such a building that is carrying on from the fall of man to the end of the world.[37]

'Like an house or temple that is building': the imagery of course is biblical, as Christians are now the temple of the Holy Spirit. God had promised to build David a temple, and we are now that temple (2 Sam. 7:11; 1 Cor. 3:16–17; 6:19).[38] When redemption is understood in the larger and all-encompassing sense outlined by Edwards, making sense

---

[37] Ibid. 121.
[38] Cf. Beale 2004. For a critique of Beale, now see DeJong 2011: 137–146.

of works, obedience and faithfulness becomes much less onerous. God is engaging in a long-term project of forming a temple. The *ultimate* temple is of course his people, with God dwelling in their midst. And it is only fitting that this more ultimate temple, as the dwelling place of the triune creator of the universe, would, over time, become an ever more fitting dwelling place for the God of holy Scripture. And as acting, moral creatures, it is to be expected that such would, over time, be marked by Spirit-induced and grace-driven works, obedience and faithfulness.

Conclusion

In this chapter I have attempted to work through key themes that throughout this book have needed more attention. First, I attempted to make sense of some of the thorny issues related to Adam, the garden and the nature of his obedience and disobedience. It is best to see the original God–Adam relationship as fundamentally gracious. There was indeed a 'legal principle' of sorts (obedience was commanded and expected, and there were consequences upon disobedience), but not necessarily a covenant of works (as this is understood by many). Adam was meant to 'advance' in some way, and just as his obedience would in no way have annulled the moral responsibility of his progeny, of those in Adam, likewise Jesus' obedience in no way annuls the moral responsibility of those who are in him.

Secondly, and related to the first point, it was suggested that Christ was the obedient one, and as the obedient one he obeyed on our behalf. But Jesus' obedience *for* me does not mean my obedience is rendered meaningless. On the contrary, since Christ is being formed in those who are his, Christ's obedience *for* his people leads to the obedience of those who are in him. Christ is the Law-Keeper, and those who are in him are there *because of his obedience and because he is being formed in his people*, lower-case 'k' Law-keepers. Our works, obedience and faithfulness are imperfect, riddled with impure motives and all the rest. Nonetheless, Christ is being formed in his people, and thus we should expect to see works, obedience and faithfulness in the people of God.

Thirdly, inaugurated eschatology is the key to the whole affair. There has been a major historical-redemptive shift in the first century with the life, death, burial, resurrection, ascension and exaltation of Jesus, and with the sending of the Holy Spirit. This nexus of events is the pivotal point in the history of redemption. The last days have begun and the people of God are being conformed to the image of the Son. But this transformation is ongoing, so we should expect to see God's people being changed (and hence the people of God *should*, and to some degree *will*, be marked by works, obedience and faithfulness). However, as we live in this in-between time, we should not be surprised to see fits and starts as God's people are gradually conformed to the image of the Son.

Fourthly, I concluded with key insights from Jonathan Edwards. As long as 'redemption' is restricted to the forgiveness of sins achieved through what took place on the cross, or perhaps to the initiation of salvation (e.g. especially justification), it will probably be hard to give full weight to the importance of works, obedience and faithfulness – *since evangelicals are passionately (and rightly!) committed to the centrality of redemption.* Edwards reminds us that redemption – in its broader sense – includes the building of the ultimate temple, the transformed people of God with whom God dwells. But when redemption is construed in this broader sense of human and cosmic transformation (one of the senses advocated by Edwards), then we begin to see the proper place of works, obedience and faithfulness in the Christian life.

Epilogue

It is high time to bring things to a close, to summarize my argument in a succinct and clear manner. We have covered a lot of ground in trying to make sense of the place of works, obedience and faithfulness in the Christian life. Let me briefly summarize the heart of the argument.

In chapter 1 I outlined a number of different strands in the New Testament where it becomes abundantly clear that works, obedience and faithfulness are simply part and parcel of the Christian life. Works, obedience and faithfulness seem at times to be *necessary*, and it is important to tease out such necessity carefully. To know Jesus is to obey him; there appears to be some sort of conditional component to our ultimate salvation; Christians must be marked by 'overcoming'; it is *necessary* that Christians have a great righteousness, and that we forgive others; the 'righteous requirement' of the law will be met in the believer; it is God who works in the believer to will and to work for his good pleasure; it is seemingly required that the believer put to death the deeds of the body; at times 'faith', 'obedience' and 'works' seem to be virtually synonyms; there is some sort of future judgment or justification according to works; there is an obedience that is an obedience of faith; we were created for good works; biblical faith is a faith that works through love. All of these strands compelled us to try to understand the centrality of works, obedience and faithfulness in the Christian life.

In chapter 2 I tried to accomplish several things. First, I argued that there is in the Old Testament, particularly in Jeremiah and Ezekiel (and ancillary passages), a pattern of looking forward to a day when there will be Spirit-induced and God-caused obedience from the heart. We found that Jeremiah 31:31–34 and Ezekiel 36:26–28 were central, and that such prophetic passages consistently point forward to a day when God's people will obey the Lord from the heart. Secondly, I turned to the New Testament to show that New Testament writers saw the new covenant as a first-century reality that has broken into history in the ministry of Jesus. I also tried to argue that at a number of points New Testament writers are explicitly or implicitly picking up on the themes we saw in Jeremiah and Ezekiel – there is a future day coming when there will be Spirit-induced and God-caused obedience from the heart among God's people. And at a number of points the New Testament writers seem to assume – if not explicitly teach – that such prophetic realities are at work in the first century.

In chapter 3 I broached some key issues relating to old and new covenant, and the relationship of law and grace. Using both older and more contemporary writers as my interlocutors, I argued several things. First, in coming to terms with the old covenant and the new, it is best to affirm both a *quantitative* and *qualitative* change in the covenants. In relation to this, it is best to see the cross of Christ as the fount of redemption and forgiveness across the entire history of redemption. Thus Old Testament believers and New Testament believers are alike saved by the grace of God manifest in the death, burial and resurrection of Jesus. Nonetheless, since Old Testament saints experience such new covenant grace *before* the actual death of Christ, we should affirm that such experience of the grace of God was somewhat proleptic. Thus only after Christ has offered himself can new covenant grace be experienced in the fuller sense. Secondly, while there is both continuity and discontinuity across the Christian canon, we need not posit a radical law–gospel contrast. With Henri Blocher and others, it is best to see the grace of God as running throughout the entire history of redemption, although exactly construing the nature of the various continuities and discontinuities is not always an easy task.

In chapter 4 I tried to work out the relationship between (1) the atoning work of Christ and (2) our works, obedience and faithfulness. It is certainly the case that the cross is the fount of our forgiveness, justification, reconciliation and redemption. Such truths must be affirmed. There is also a clear pattern in the New Testament in which the cross leads to human transformation and sanctification. That is, the gospel is the power of God unto salvation, and one of the things we see clearly in the New Testament is that the cross is not *only* the means of our initial entry into a covenant relationship with God. The cross is also that from which our growth in holiness proceeds. Thus a work that is *outside* and *for* us is also something that leads to our transformation. Jesus dies for his people, not *simply* so that they may be 'initially' saved. He dies for his bride because what he is doing is setting in motion a process by which his bride might be purified and presented *back* to him as his bride – without blemish.

The cross is central to the whole process of redemption – its beginning, continuation and completion.

In chapter 5 I argued that key to the whole affair of making sense of works, obedience and faithfulness in Christ is union with him. I proposed – with John Murray – that union with Christ is the grid through which we make sense of the whole biblical teaching on redemption. It is in coming to terms with union with Christ that we continued to bump into the issue of divine and human agency, for when we think through union with Christ we are forced to recognize that the destiny of the Christian is so bound up with the destiny of Jesus that it is impossible to separate the two. Thus, while it is *I* who obey, it is at the same time *Christ in me* who is at work. As we come to terms with union with Christ, we see that, since he is being formed in us, true – if marred, impartial, and so on – obedience characterizes us.

In chapter 6 I tried to face squarely the thorny issue of judgment according to works, and a future aspect of justification. While all true Protestants are always seeking to improve their understanding of *sola fide*, and to sharpen the best way to understand and express the teaching of holy writ (i.e. we should be a people engaged in the project of *semper reformanda*, 'always to be reformed'), I remain unpersuaded that the traditional affirmation of justification by faith alone is in need of major renovation or adjustment. Is there always more to learn? Certainly. Better ways to express a particular biblical teaching? Undoubtedly. But the willingness to rethink central doctrines and tenets does not entail that one never arrives at conclusions, or that one should be dismissed out of hand for believing that the Reformational understanding of justification by faith alone apart from works is worthy of attention and affirmation.

It is at the same time necessary to deal squarely with a *future* component of justification, and to come to terms with how works relate to such a future aspect of justification, and to understand properly Scripture's teaching on justification according to works. After looking at key texts, and after engaging at some length with interlocutors both older and more contemporary, I argued that we indeed must affirm that works have a crucial place at the judgment, and that works play a role in a future aspect of justification. There is no reason to gloss over these truths, and we discovered that there is a rich tradition of Reformational thinkers (including Calvin himself) who dealt with these issues at great length. I attempted to summarize and engage fairly with the perspective of N. T. Wright. As many brilliant insights as this senior scholar has, I demurred from embracing his construal. When all is said and done, the basic structure of an older Reformational understanding, including the insights of persons like Calvin still proves helpful and compelling.

Lastly, in chapter 7 I tried to bring some strands together, and to devote space to some of the key insights that may help hold together the many issues faced in this monograph. First, I returned to the question of Adam and the garden, and the nature of his obedience and disobedience. It is best to see the original God–Adam relationship as fundamentally gracious. There is indeed a 'legal principle', but it is unnecessary to posit a 'covenant of works' into the original God–Adam relationship. With Henri Blocher I argued that it is essential to grasp that there is a fundamental 'advance' in the history of redemption as one moves from old covenant to new. This is best seen as both a *quantitative* and a *qualitative* difference between old and new covenants. Secondly, I returned to the importance of linking *my obedience* to *Christ's obedience*. We are here back to questions of divine and human agency and union with Christ, who obeys *for me* and *in my place*. But rather than seeing Christ's obedience as something that renders my obedience superfluous, his obedience should be seen as the fount or source of obedience, for Christ is being formed in me. Thirdly, I argued that inaugurated eschatology is the key to grasping the *real* but *imperfect* nature of my works, obedience and faithfulness. Fourthly, I leaned on Jonathan Edwards, who so powerfully argued that there is both a 'narrower' and 'broader' way of thinking about redemption. Both are needed. When we think of redemption as including human and cosmic transformation, *and when we properly root such redemption in the precious reality of the gospel itself*, we are able to affirm (as we should!) the cherished insights of the gospel of Christ crucified, while giving full weight to the clear biblical teaching that the true people of God will indeed be marked by works, obedience and faithfulness.

Bibliography

Alexander, T. D. (1994), 'Abraham Re-Assessed Theologically: The Abrahamic Narrative and the New Testament', in R. S. Hess, G. J. Wenham and P. E. Satterthwaite (eds.), *He Swore an Oath: Biblical Themes from Genesis 12–50*, Carlisle: Paternoster; Grand Rapids: Baker, 7–28.

Allen, R. M., and D. J. Treier (2008), 'Dogmatic Theology and Biblical Perspectives on Justification: A Reply to Leithart', *WTJ* 70: 105–110.

Athanasius (1952), 'Four Discourses Against the Arians', tr. J. H. Newman and A. Robertson, in P. Schaff and H. Wace (eds.), *A Select Library of Nicene and Post-Nicene Fathers of the Christian Church: Second Series*, Grand Rapids: Eerdmans, 303–447.

Augustine (1991), *Confessions*, ed. and tr. H. Chadwick, Oxford: Oxford University Press.

——— (1994), 'Sermon 333', in *Sermons (306–340A) on the Saints*, ed. J. E. Rotelle, O.S.A., tr. E. Hill, O.P., vol. 3.9 of *The Works of Saint Augustine: A Translation for the 21st Century*, New Rochelle, N.Y.: New City, 198–203.

——— (1999), 'Grace and Free Choice', in R. J. Teske, S.J. (ed. and tr.), *Answer to the Pelagians IV*, vol. 1.26 of *The Works of Saint Augustine: A Translation for the 21st Century*, New Rochelle, N.Y.: New City Press, 70–107.

Aune, D. (1998), *Revelation 6–16*, WBC 52B, Nashville: Thomas Nelson.

Barclay, J. M. G. (2006), '"By the Grace of God I am What I am": Grace and Agency in Philo and Paul', in J. M. G. Barclay and S. J. Gathercole (eds.), *Divine and Human Agency in Paul and His Cultural Environment*, New York: T. & T. Clark, 140–157.

Barnett, P. (1997), *The Second Epistle to the Corinthians*, NICNT, Grand Rapids: Eerdmans.

Barth, K. (1962), *Church Dogmatics*, ed. and tr. G. W. Bromiley and T. F. Torrance, 4 vols., Edinburgh: T. & T. Clark.

Bauckham, R. (1993), *The Climax of Prophecy*, Edinburgh: T. & T. Clark.

Beale, G. K. (2004), *The Temple and the Church's Mission: A Biblical Theology of the Dwelling Place of God*, NSBT 17, Leicester: Apollos; Downers Grove: InterVarsity Press.

————— (2011), *A New Testament Biblical Theology: The Unfolding of the Old Testament in the New*, Grand Rapids: Baker; Nottingham: Apollos.

Berkouwer, G. C. (1952), *Faith and Sanctification*, Studies in Dogmatics, Grand Rapids: Eerdmans.

Billings, T. (2011), *Union with Christ: Reframing Theology and Ministry for the Church*, Grand Rapids: Baker.

Blocher, H. (1975), *Songs of the Servant: Isaiah's Good News*, Leicester: Inter-Varsity Press.

————— (1987), 'The "Analogy of Faith" in the Study of Scripture: In Search of Justification and Guide-lines', *SBET* 5: 17–38.

————— (2001), *La Doctrine du péché et de la rédemption*, Didaskalia, Vaux-sur-Seine: Edifac.

————— (2004), 'Justification of the Ungodly (*Sola Fide*): Theological Reflections', in D. A. Carson, P. T. O'Brien and M. A. Seifrid (eds.), *Justification and Variegated Nomism: The Paradoxes of Paul*, Grand Rapids: Baker, 465–500.

————— (2006), 'Old Covenant, New Covenant', in A. T. B. McGowan (ed.), *Always Reforming: Explorations in Systematic Theology*, Leicester: Apollos; Downers Grove: InterVarsity Press, 240–270.

————— (2011), 'Sanctification by Faith?', unpublished paper presented at Fourteenth Edinburgh Conference on Christian Dogmatics, 1 Sept. 2011.

Block, D. I. (1989), 'The Prophet of the Spirit: The Use of RWH in the Book of Ezekiel', *JETS* 32: 27–49.

Bray, G. (1983), 'The *Filioque* Clause in History and Theology', *TynB* 34: 91–144.

————— (2011), *Galatians, Ephesians*, RCS, Downers Grove: InterVarsity Press.

Bruce, F. F. (1997), *The Epistle to the Hebrews*, NICNT, Grand Rapids: Eerdmans.

Caird, G. B. (1966), *A Commentary on the Revelation of St. John the Divine*, BNTC, London: A. & C. Black.

Calvin, J. (1851), *The True Method of Giving Peace, and of Reforming the Church*, tr. Henry Beveridge, Edinburgh: Calvin Translation Society.

————— (1960), *Institutes of the Christian Religion*, ed. J. T. McNeill, tr. F. L. Battles, Philadelphia: Westminster.

—————— (1979), *Commentary on the Gospel According to John*, tr. W. Pringle, in *Calvin's Commentaries*, 22 vols., Edinburgh: Calvin Translation Society, 1847; repr. Grand Rapids: Baker.

—————— (1981), *Calvin's Commentaries*, Edinburgh: Calvin Translation Society, 1844–56, repr. in 22 volumes, Grand Rapids: Baker.

Carson, D. A. (1984), 'Matthew', in F. E. Gaebelein (ed.), EBC 8, Grand Rapids: Eerdmans.

—————— (2004), '"You Have No Need That Anyone Should Teach You" (1 John 2:27): An Old Testament Allusion That Determines the Interpretation', in P. J. Williams, A. D. Clarke, P. M. Head and D. Instone-Brewer (eds.), *The New Testament in Its First Century Setting: Essays on Context and Background in Honour of B. W. Winter on His 65th Birthday*, Grand Rapids: Eerdmans, 269–280.

Clark, R. S. (2007), *Covenant, Justification, and Pastoral Ministry: Essays by the Faculty of Westminster Seminary California*, Phillipsburg: P. & R.

DeJong, B. (2011), 'On Earth as It Is in Heaven: The Pastoral Typology of James B. Jordan', in P. J. Leithart and J. Barach (eds.), *The Glory of Kings: A Festschrift in Honor of James B. Jordan*, Eugene, Ore.: Pickwick, 133–146.

Dumbrell, W. J. (1994), *The Search for Order: Biblical Eschatology in Focus*, Grand Rapids: Baker.

—————— (2005), *Romans: A New Covenant Commentary*, Eugene, Ore.: Wipf & Stock.

Dunn, J. D. G. (1988), *Romans 1–8*, WBC 38A, Dallas: Word.

Edwards, J. (1989), *A History of the Work of Redemption*, The Works of Jonathan Edwards, vol. 9, ed. J. F. Wilson, New Haven: Yale University Press.

—————— (2000), *The 'Miscellanies' 501–832*, The Works of Jonathan Edwards, vol. 18, ed. A. Chamberlain, New Haven: Yale University Press.

Engelbrecht, E. A. (2011), *Friends of the Law: Luther's Use of the Law for the Christian Life*, St. Louis: Concordia.

Frame, John (2002), 'Law and Gospel' <http://www.frame-poythress.org/law-and-gospel>, accessed 27 Apr. 2013.

—————— (2008), *The Doctrine of the Christian Life* (A Theology of Lordship), Phillipsburg, N.J.: P. & R.

—————— (2011), 'Meredith G. Kline's *Kingdom Prologue*', in *The Escondido Theology: A Reformed Response to Two Kingdom Theology*, Lakeland, Fla.: Whitefield Media, 151–198.

Gaffin Jr., R. B. (2002), 'Redemption and Resurrection: An Exercise in Biblical-Systematic Theology', *Them* 27: 16–31.

——— (2006), *By Faith, Not by Sight: Paul and the Order of Salvation*, Oakhill School of Theology Series, Bletchley: Paternoster.

Gathercole, S. J. (2002a), 'A Law unto Themselves: The Gentiles in Romans 2.14–15 Revisited', *JSNT* 85: 27–49.

——— (2002b), *Where Is Boasting? Early Jewish Soteriology and Paul's Response in Romans 1–5*, Grand Rapids: Eerdmans.

Gatiss, L. (2013), 'Adoring the Fullness of the Scriptures in John Owen's Commentary on Hebrews', PhD diss., Cambridge: University of Cambridge.

Hafemann, S. J. (1990), *Suffering and Ministry in the Spirit: Paul's Defense of His Ministry in II Corinthians 2:14–3:3*, Grand Rapids: Eerdmans.

——— (1995), *Paul, Moses, and the History of Israel: The Letter/Spirit Contrast and the Argument from Scripture in 2 Corinthians 3*, WUNT 81, Tübingen: Mohr Siebeck.

——— (1997), 'The Spirit of the New Covenant, the Law, and the Temple of God's Presence: Five Theses on Qumran Self-Understanding and the Contours of Paul's Thought', in J. Ådna, S. J. Hafemann and O. Hofius (eds.), *Evangelium Schriftauslegung Kirche: Festschrift für Peter Stuhlmacher zum 65. Geburtstag*, Göttingen: Vandenhoeck & Ruprecht, 172–189.

——— (2000), *2 Corinthians*, NIVAC, Grand Rapids: Zondervan.

——— (2007), 'The Covenant Relationship', in S. J. Hafemann and P. R. House (eds.), *Central Themes in Biblical Theology: Mapping Unity in Diversity*, Nottingham: Apollos; Grand Rapids: Baker, 20–65.

——— (n.d.), 'Faith, Hope, and Love' course notebook, South Hamilton, Mass.: Gordon-Conwell Theological Seminary.

Hagner, D. A. (1993), *Matthew 1–13*, WBC 33A, Dallas: Word.

Hamilton Jr., J. M. (2006), *God's Indwelling Presence: The Holy Spirit in the Old and New Testaments*, NACSBT 1, Nashville: B. & H. Academic.

Harris, M. J. (1978), 'Prepositions in New Testament Theology', *NIDNTT* 3: 1170–1215.

——— (2012), *Prepositions and Theology in the Greek New Testament: An Essential Reference Resource for Exegesis*, Grand Rapids: Eerdmans.

Heen, E. M., and P. D. W. Krey (2005), *Hebrews*, ACCS, Downers Grove: InterVarsity Press.

Hodge, C. (1953), *Commentary on the Epistle to the Romans*, rev. ed. Grand Rapids: Eerdmans.

—— (1993), *Romans*, CCC, Wheaton: Crossway.

Horton, M. S. (2007), 'Which Covenant Theology?', in R. S. Clark (ed.), *Covenant, Justification, and Pastoral Ministry: Essays by the Faculty of Westminster Seminary California*, Phillipsburg, N.J.: P. & R., 197–227.

Karlberg, M. W. (2007), Review of P. A. Rainbow, *The Way of Salvation: The Role of Christian Obedience in Justification*, and R. B. Gaffin Jr., *By Faith, Not by Sight: Paul and the Order of Salvation*, *JETS* 50: 423–428.

Kline, M. G. (2006), *Kingdom Prologue: Genesis Foundations for a Covenantal Worldview*, Eugene, Ore.: Wipf & Stock.

Laato, T. (1997), 'Justification According to James: A Comparison with Paul', *TrinJ* 18.1: 43–84.

Ladd, G. E. (1972), *A Commentary on the Revelation of John*, Grand Rapids: Eerdmans.

—— (1993), *A Theology of the New Testament*, rev. ed., Grand Rapids: Eerdmans.

Leithart, P. (2007), 'Justification as Verdict and Deliverance: A Biblical Perspective', *ProEccl* 16: 56–72.

—— (2011), *Athanasius*, Foundations of Theological Exegesis and Christian Spirituality, Grand Rapids: Baker.

Letham, R. (2009), *The Westminster Assembly: Reading Its Theology in Historical Context*, Phillipsburg, N.J.: P. & R.

Lillback, P. A. (2007), 'Calvin's Development of the Doctrine of Forensic Justification: Calvin and the Early Lutherans on Relationship of Justification and Renewal', in K. S. Oliphint (ed.), *Justified in Christ: God's Plan for Us in Justification*, ed. K. S. Oliphint, Fearn, Scotland: Mentor, Christian Focus, 51–80.

Lloyd-Jones, D. M. (1973), *Romans: An Exposition of Chapters 7:1–8:4, The Law: Its Functions and Limits*, Edinburgh: Banner of Truth.

Luther, M. (1962), 'Two Kinds of Righteousness', in J. Dillenberger, *Martin Luther: Selections from His Writings*, New York: Doubleday, 86–96.

McCartney, D. G. (2009), *James*, BECNT, Grand Rapids: Baker.

McGowan, A. T. B. (2005), 'In Defence of "Headship Theology"', in J. A. Grant and A. I. Wilson (eds.), *The God of Covenant: Biblical, Theological, and Contemporary Perspectives*, Leicester: Apollos, 178–199.

Moo, D. J. (1985), *James*, TNTC, Leicester: Inter-Varsity Press.

—— (1991), *Romans 1–8*, WEC, Chicago: Moody.

—— (1996), *The Epistle of Paul to the Romans*, NICNT, Grand Rapids: Eerdmans.

—— (2007), 'The Obedience of Faith', unpublished plenary address, Evangelical Theological Society Annual Meeting, 14 Nov. 2007.

Moon, J. N. (2011), *Jeremiah's New Covenant: An Augustinian Reading*, JTIS 3, Winona Lake: Eisenbrauns.

Morris, L. (1992), *The Gospel According to Matthew*, PNTC, Grand Rapids: Eerdmans; Leicester: Apollos.

Mounce, R. H. (1977), *The Book of Revelation*, NICNT, Grand Rapids: Eerdmans.

Muller, R. A. (1985), *Dictionary of Latin and Greek Theological Terms: Drawn Principally from Protestant Scholastic Theology*, Grand Rapids: Baker.

Murray, J. (1955), *Redemption Accomplished and Applied*, Grand Rapids: Eerdmans.

—— (1959), *The Epistle to the Romans; The English Text with Introduction, Exposition, and Notes*, vol. 1, Grand Rapids: Eerdmans.

Murray, S. R. (2002), *Law, Life, and the Living God: The Third Use of the Law in Modern American Lutheranism*, St. Louis: Concordia.

O'Brien, P. T. (1999), *The Letter to the Ephesians*, PNTC, Grand Rapids: Eerdmans; Leicester: Apollos.

—— (2010), *The Letter to the Hebrews*, PNTC, Grand Rapids: Eerdmans; Leicester: Apollos.

Oden, T. C. (1990), *After Modernity . . . What? Agenda for Theology*, Grand Rapids: Zondervan.

Owen, J. (1661), Θεολογούμενα Παντοδαπά, sive, De Natura, Ortu Progressu, et Studio Verae Theologiae [Theologoumena Pantodapa], Oxford.

Owen, J. (1965), *The Works of John Owen*, W. H. Gould (ed.), 16 vols., London: Banner of Truth Trust.

—— (1991), *An Exposition of the Epistle to the Hebrews: With Preliminary Exercitations*, ed. W. H. Gould, Edinburgh: Banner of Truth Trust.

—— (2006), *The Doctrine of Justification by Faith Through the Imputation of the Righteousness of Christ Explained, Confirmed, and Vindicated*, Grand Rapids: Reformation Heritage.

—— (2007), *Communion with God*, Fearn, Scotland: Christian Focus.

Packer, J. I. (2003), 'Introduction', in J. Owen, *The Mortification of Sin: A Puritan's View of How to Deal with Sin in Your Life*, Fearn, Scotland: Christian Focus.

Peterson, D. (1995), *Possessed by God: A New Testament Theology of Sanctification and Holiness*, NSBT 1, Leicester: Apollos.

——— (2012), *Transformed by God: New Covenant Life and Ministry*, Leicester: Inter-Varsity Press; Downers Grove: InterVarsity Press.

Piper, J. (1995), *Future Grace*, Leicester: Inter-Varsity Press; Colorado Springs: Multnomah.

——— (2002), *Counted Righteous in Christ: Should We Abandon the Imputation of Christ's Righteousness?*, Wheaton: Crossway; Leicester: Inter-Varsity Press.

——— (2007), *The Future of Justification: A Response to N. T. Wright*, Wheaton: Crossway; Leicester: Inter-Varsity Press.

Rainbow, P. (2005), *The Way of Salvation: The Role of Christian Obedience in Justification*, Milton Keynes: Paternoster.

Reinmuth, E. (1985), *Geist und Gesetz: Studien zu Voraussetzungen und Inhalt der paulinischen Paränese*, Berlin: Evangelisch Verlagsanstalt.

Rendtorff, R. (1998), *The Covenant Formula: An Exegetical and Theological Investigation*, Edinburgh: T. & T. Clark.

Robertson, O. P. (1980), *The Christ of the Covenants*, Grand Rapids: Baker.

Rosner, B. S. (2013), *Paul and the Law: Keeping the Commandments of God*, NSBT 32, Nottingham: Apollos; Downers Grove: InterVarsity Press.

Ryle, J. C. (2002), *Holiness*, in J. I. Packer (ed.), *Faithfulness and Holiness: The Witness of J.C. Ryle*, Wheaton: Crossway, 91–246.

Sandlin, P. A. (2007), *A Faith That Is Never Alone: A Response to Westminster Seminary California*, La Grange, Calif.: Kerygma.

Sarcerius, Erasmus (1542), *In epistolas Divi Pauli ad Galatas et Ephesios annotationes*, ad Eph. 5:26, Frankfurt.

Schreiner, T. (1993a), 'Did Paul Believe in Justification by Works? Another Look at Romans 2', *BBR* 31: 131–158.

——— (1993b), 'Works of the Law', in G. F. Hawthorne and R. P. Martin (eds.), *Dictionary of Paul and His Letters*, Downers Grove: InterVarsity Press; Leicester: Inter-Varsity Press, 975–979.

——— (1998), *Romans*, BECNT, Grand Rapids: Baker.

——— (2001), *Paul, Apostle of God's Glory in Christ: A Pauline Theology*, Downers Grove: InterVarsity Press; Leicester: Apollos.

———— (2007), 'The Commands of God', in S. J. Hafemann and P. R. House (eds.), *Central Themes in Biblical Theology: Mapping Unity in Diversity*, Nottingham: Apollos; Grand Rapids: Baker, 66–101.

———— (2008), *New Testament Theology: Magnifying God in Christ*, Grand Rapids: Baker; Nottingham: Apollos.

Shepherd, N. (2007), 'The Imputation of Active Obedience', in P. A. Sandlin (ed.), *A Faith That Is Never Alone: A Response to Westminster Seminary California*, La Grange, Calif.: Kerygma, 249–278.

Sprinkle, P. M. (2008), *Law and Life: The Interpretation of Leviticus 18:5 in Early Judaism and in Paul*, WUNT 2.241, Tübingen: Mohr Siebeck.

Stanley, S. K. (1995), 'A New Covenant Hermeneutic: The Use of Scripture in Hebrews 8–10', PhD thesis, Sheffield: University of Sheffield.

Stuhlmacher, P. (1994), *Paul's Letter to the Romans: A Commentary*, Louisville: Westminster John Knox.

Trueman, C. R. (2007), *John Owen: Reformed Catholic, Renaissance Man*, Aldershot: Ashgate.

Turretin, F. (1997), *Institutes of Elenctic Theology*, vol. 2, Phillipsburg, N.J.: P. & R.

Vos, G. (1952), *The Pauline Eschatology*, Grand Rapids: Eerdmans.

———— (1954), *Biblical Theology, Old and New Testament*, Grand Rapids: Eerdmans.

———— (1980a), 'The Alleged Legalism in Paul's Doctrine of Justification', in R. B. Gaffin Jr. (ed.), *Redemptive History and Biblical Interpretation: The Shorter Writings of Geerhardus Vos*, Phillipsburg, N.J.: P. & R., 383–399.

———— (1980b), 'Hebrews, the Epistle of the Diatheke', in R. B. Gaffin Jr. (ed.), *Redemptive History and Biblical Interpretation: The Shorter Writings of Geerhardus Vos*, Phillipsburg, N.J.: P. & R., 161–233.

Wright, N. T. (1997), *What Saint Paul Really Said: Was Paul of Tarsus the Real Founder of Christianity?*, Grand Rapids: Eerdmans.

———— (2001), 'The Shape of Justification: A Misunderstood Term Has Caused Great Confusion in Understanding Paul and It's Time to Get It Right', *BRev* 17.2: 8, 50.

———— (2006), 'New Perspectives on Paul', in B. L. McCormack (ed.), *Justification in Perspective: Historical Developments and Contemporary Challenges*, Grand Rapids: Baker; Edinburgh: Rutherford House, 243–264.

———— (2009), *Justification: God's Plan and Paul's Vision*, Downers Grove: InterVarsity Press.

Index of authors

Index of Scripture references